Hiring Sales Winners

The Ultimate Guide to Hiring TOP Performing Sales Talent!

Gerard Assey

Hiring Sales Winners
The Ultimate Guide to Hiring
TOP Performing Sales Talent!
By
Gerard Assey
© Copyright 2023 by Author

Published by:
Gerard Assey
19/18, Palli Arasan Street
Anna Nagar East
Chennai - 600 102

ISBN: 978-93-92492-40-2

(Courtesy Anna Shvets- https://www.pexels.com- Thank you!)

Table of Contents

Preface

Welcome to **'Hiring Sales Winners:** *The Ultimate Guide to Hiring Top Performing Sales Talent!'*- a valuable resource for organizations and hiring managers who are determined to build a high-performing sales team and achieve exceptional sales results.

In today's competitive business landscape, hiring top sales professionals is crucial for sustainable growth and success. However, the process of identifying, attracting, and selecting the right talent can be challenging and time-consuming. That's where this guide comes in.

The purpose of this book is to provide you with a comprehensive framework and practical strategies to streamline your sales hiring process and ensure that you are bringing on board the best sales talent available. It covers every aspect of hiring sales professionals, from understanding the impact of top performers to creating effective job descriptions, conducting interviews, making compelling offers, on-boarding new hires, and retaining top talent.

Throughout the chapters, you will find valuable insights, expert advice, and actionable tips that you can implement immediately. Real-life examples and case studies will illustrate how these strategies have been successfully applied in different industries and organizations.

'Hiring Sales Winners' is designed to be your go-to resource, whether you are new to hiring or seeking to improve your existing processes. It is a practical guide that will help you navigate the complex world of sales recruitment and make informed decisions at every stage of the hiring journey.

Remember, hiring top performing sales talent is a continuous process of improvement and adaptation. The strategies presented in this book are not one-size-fits-all, but rather a foundation upon which you can build and customize your own unique approach.

I encourage you to read this book with an open mind, embracing the principles and strategies that resonate with your organization's goals and culture. Take the knowledge gained and apply it to your hiring practices, making adjustments along the way to suit your specific needs and challenges.

I wish you great success in your quest to hire sales winners who will drive your organization's growth and success.

May this guide empower you to make confident hiring decisions and build a winning sales team that exceeds expectations.

Chapter 1
Introduction to Hiring Sales Professionals

Introduction to Hiring Sales Professionals

In today's competitive business landscape, the role of sales professionals has become increasingly vital for the success and growth of organizations across industries. In this section, we delve into why hiring sales professionals matters and the significant impact they can have on a company's performance and bottom line.

Why Hiring Sales Professionals Matters
The Importance of Sales Professionals: Sales professionals serve as the front line of a company's revenue generation efforts. They are responsible for driving sales, acquiring new customers, building relationships, and ultimately contributing to the company's financial success. By hiring skilled and effective sales professionals, organizations can gain a competitive edge in the market.
Revenue Generation: Sales professionals play a pivotal role in generating revenue for a company. They are responsible for identifying potential customers, understanding their needs, presenting compelling solutions, and closing deals. Effective sales professionals can consistently meet or exceed sales targets, leading to increased revenue and profitability for the organization.
Customer Acquisition and Retention: Sales professionals are instrumental in acquiring new customers and expanding the customer base. Their ability to build relationships, understand customer pain points, and effectively communicate the value of products or services plays a crucial role in attracting

and retaining customers. Hiring talented sales professionals can result in higher customer acquisition rates and enhanced customer loyalty.

Market Expansion: Sales professionals possess the skills and knowledge to explore new markets and expand the organization's reach. With their expertise in market research, competitor analysis, and relationship building, they can identify untapped opportunities and drive business growth. Hiring sales professionals who excel at market expansion can open doors to new customers, partnerships, and revenue streams.

Building Strong Sales Teams: Hiring sales professionals is not just about individual contributions but also about building a high-performing sales team. Top-performing sales professionals bring valuable experience, leadership qualities, and a competitive spirit that can inspire and motivate their teammates. A strong sales team fosters a collaborative environment, encourages healthy competition, and elevates the overall sales culture within the organization.

Representing the Company: Sales professionals are often the face of the company, interacting directly with clients and prospects. They embody the organization's values, brand, and reputation. Hiring sales professionals who align with the company's vision and values ensures that they will represent the organization effectively, enhancing its image and credibility in the marketplace.

Hiring sales professionals is a strategic investment that directly impacts a company's revenue generation, customer acquisition and retention, market expansion, and overall sales team performance. By recognizing the importance of hiring sales professionals, organizations can prioritize finding top talent, fostering a culture of excellence, and positioning themselves for long-term success in a competitive business environment.

The Impact of Top Performing Sales Talent

We will now delve into the profound impact that top-performing sales talent can have on an organization, by exploring the qualities and abilities that set them apart from average sales professionals- how their contributions can drive exceptional results and propel a company to new heights.

Differentiating Top Performers: Top performing sales professionals consistently exceed expectations and deliver outstanding results. They possess a unique combination of skills, traits, and experiences that make them highly effective in their roles. These individuals excel in areas such as prospecting, building relationships, negotiation, closing deals, and maintaining customer loyalty. They have a deep understanding of the sales process and can adapt to various selling situations with ease.

Driving Revenue Growth: Top performers have a direct impact on revenue generation. Their exceptional sales skills and ability to navigate complex deals enable them to close high-value contracts and achieve ambitious sales targets. By consistently surpassing revenue goals, top sales professionals contribute to the financial success of the organization and create a positive ripple effect throughout the entire company.

Exceeding Sales Targets: One of the defining characteristics of top-performing sales professionals is their ability to consistently surpass sales targets and quotas. They set ambitious goals for themselves and demonstrate a relentless drive to achieve them. By exceeding targets, these individuals demonstrate their effectiveness in generating revenue, acquiring new customers, and maximizing the value of each sales opportunity.

Building Strong Customer Relationships: Top sales professionals excel in building and maintaining strong relationships with customers. They have exceptional interpersonal skills and a knack for understanding customer needs and motivations. Through effective communication, active listening, and empathy, they establish trust and credibility with clients. This results in long-lasting customer relationships, repeat business, and positive word-of-mouth referrals, which further contribute to the organization's success.

Enhancing Team Morale and Collaboration: The presence of top-performing sales talent within a team can have a significant positive impact on overall morale and collaboration. Their success serves as a source of inspiration and motivation for their colleagues, driving healthy competition and elevating performance standards. They often share their knowledge, best practices, and strategies, contributing to the collective growth and development of the entire sales team.

Influencing Company Culture: Top sales professionals, through their exceptional performance and dedication, can shape and enhance the sales culture within an organization. Their work ethic, professionalism, and commitment to excellence can inspire others to strive for greatness. They set a high standard of performance and foster an environment that encourages continuous improvement, innovation, and a results-oriented mindset.

Top performing sales professionals possess a unique blend of skills, traits, and experiences that enable them to drive exceptional results. Their ability to consistently surpass sales targets, build strong customer relationships, enhance team morale, and influence company culture makes them invaluable assets to any organization. Recognizing the impact of top sales talent allows organizations to prioritize hiring and nurturing individuals who can make a significant difference and contribute to long-term success.

Understanding the Sales Hiring Process

Before we get into details, we will provide a comprehensive overview of the sales hiring process, by breaking down the different stages involved, from defining the hiring needs and job requirements to on-boarding the selected candidate. Understanding the sales hiring process is crucial for effectively attracting, assessing, and selecting top sales talent for your organization.

Defining Hiring Needs: The first step in the sales hiring process is to define your hiring needs. This involves identifying the specific sales roles and positions required within your organization. You should consider factors such as sales team structure, target markets, product/service offerings, and desired sales objectives. Clearly defining your hiring needs sets the foundation for the entire process.

Job Analysis and Requirements: Once you have determined your hiring needs, conduct a thorough job analysis to understand the key responsibilities, skills, and qualifications required for the sales position. This includes identifying the necessary sales experience, product knowledge, industry expertise, communication skills, and other relevant competencies. Developing a detailed job description based on this analysis will help attract candidates who possess the desired qualifications.

Sourcing Candidates: The next step is to source potential candidates for the sales position. This can be done through various channels, including online job boards, professional networks, industry-specific platforms, and recruitment agencies. You can also leverage social media platforms and employee referrals to expand your candidate pool. A proactive approach to sourcing will increase your chances of finding top sales talent.

Resume Screening: Once you have received a pool of resumes, conduct a thorough screening process to shortlist qualified candidates. Evaluate resumes based on the desired qualifications and experience outlined in the job description. Look for indicators of past sales success, relevant achievements, and consistency in career progression. Narrow down the candidate pool to those who meet the initial criteria.

Interviewing: The interviewing stage is critical for assessing the suitability of candidates for the sales role. Conduct structured interviews that focus on both behavioral and situational questions to gauge the candidates' sales skills, problem-solving abilities, communication, and relationship-building skills. Additionally, consider including role-play scenarios or case studies to observe their approach to sales situations.

Assessments and Tests: To gain deeper insights into candidates' sales abilities, consider incorporating assessments and tests into the hiring process. This may include sales simulations, personality assessments, cognitive ability tests, or sales aptitude evaluations. These assessments can provide a more objective evaluation of candidates' sales capabilities and help identify the best fit for the role.

Reference and Background Checks: Before making a final decision, conduct thorough reference and background checks on the shortlisted candidates. Contact previous employers, colleagues, or clients to gain insights into the candidate's work ethic, performance, and interpersonal skills. Verify their educational qualifications and any claims made during the hiring process.

Offer and Negotiation: Once you have identified the top candidate, make a job offer that includes competitive compensation, benefits, and any other relevant incentives. Be prepared to negotiate and discuss terms to ensure a mutually beneficial agreement. Promptly address any concerns or questions the candidate may have and provide a clear timeline for their acceptance.

On-boarding: The final stage of the sales hiring process is on-boarding the selected candidate. Develop a comprehensive on-boarding program that includes training on products/services, sales techniques, company policies, and any specific tools or software used. Set clear expectations, establish goals, and assign mentors or coaches to support the new hire during their initial period.

Understanding the sales hiring process is crucial for finding and selecting top sales talent. By following a structured approach that encompasses defining hiring needs, conducting job analysis, sourcing candidates, screening resumes, conducting interviews and assessments, and finalizing the offer and on-boarding, you can ensure a successful hiring outcome. This comprehensive understanding of the sales hiring process will set the stage for effectively attracting and selecting top-performing sales professionals for your organization.

The Benefits of Hiring Top Sales Professionals

We will now explore how these individuals can positively impact a company's bottom line, drive revenue growth, and contribute to long-term success. Understanding the advantages of hiring top sales talent will help organizations prioritize and invest in recruiting and retaining high-performing professionals.

Driving Revenue Growth: Top sales professionals have a direct impact on revenue generation. Their exceptional sales skills, industry knowledge, and ability to build relationships enable them to consistently meet or exceed sales targets. By leveraging their expertise, top performers can identify opportunities, close high-value deals, and maximize the value of each sales opportunity. Hiring top sales talent increases the potential for revenue growth and enhances the overall financial performance of the organization.

Increasing Market Share: With their exceptional sales acumen, top sales professionals can contribute to expanding market share. By effectively positioning products or services, understanding customer needs, and tailoring solutions, they can capture a larger portion of the market. Top performers have the ability to outperform competitors, build customer loyalty, and establish the organization as a market leader.

Expanding Customer Base: Top sales professionals excel at acquiring new customers and expanding the organization's customer base. Their strong networking skills, ability to identify potential clients, and persuasive communication enable them to attract new business opportunities. By hiring top sales talent, organizations can tap into new markets, reach a wider audience, and establish fruitful customer relationships that fuel long-term growth.

Building Strong Relationships: Top sales professionals possess exceptional relationship-building skills. They can establish trust, credibility, and rapport with clients, leading to strong and loyal customer relationships. These relationships go beyond a single transaction and can result in repeat business, referrals, and long-term partnerships. By hiring top sales talent, organizations can cultivate a network of satisfied customers who become advocates for the brand.

Enhancing Sales Team Performance: Top sales professionals not only excel individually but also elevate the performance of the entire sales team. Their success serves as a benchmark for other team members and inspires them to improve and strive for excellence. Top performers often share their knowledge, best practices, and sales strategies, fostering a culture of continuous learning and improvement within the team. Hiring top sales talent creates a positive and competitive environment that motivates the entire sales team to achieve outstanding results.

Attracting More Top Talent: Organizations that consistently hire top sales professionals create a reputation for attracting and retaining high-performing talent. Top sales professionals are often sought-after individuals who value opportunities for growth, a competitive environment, and attractive compensation packages. By building a team of top performers, organizations become more attractive to other top sales professionals, allowing for a steady stream of talented candidates for future hiring needs.

Improving Sales Culture: Hiring top sales talent has a positive impact on the overall sales culture within an organization. Their professionalism, drive, and commitment to excellence set a high standard for performance and contribute to a positive and motivated sales environment. A strong sales culture fosters collaboration, healthy competition, and continuous improvement. It creates an atmosphere where sales professionals can thrive, resulting in improved sales outcomes and overall organizational success.

The benefits of hiring top sales professionals are far-reaching. They contribute to revenue growth, market share expansion, customer acquisition and retention, enhanced sales team performance, and the establishment of a strong sales culture. By recognizing and investing in top sales talent, organizations position themselves for long-term success, competitive advantage, and sustainable growth in the marketplace.

Chapter 2
Defining Your
Sales Hiring Strategy

Defining Your Sales Hiring Strategy

Assessing Your Current Sales Team

Before embarking on the journey of hiring sales professionals, it is essential to assess your current sales team and understand its strengths, weaknesses, and areas for improvement. This chapter explores the importance of evaluating your existing sales team, provides guidance on conducting a comprehensive assessment, and offers examples to illustrate the process.

Importance of Assessing Your Current Sales Team: Assessing your current sales team is a crucial step in defining your sales hiring strategy. It allows you to gain insights into the team's performance, identify gaps in skills or expertise, and determine the specific areas where new hires can make the most impact. By understanding the strengths and weaknesses of your current team, you can align your hiring strategy to address those gaps and create a well-rounded and high-performing sales force.

Conducting a Comprehensive Assessment: To assess your current sales team effectively, consider the following aspects:

1. Performance Evaluation: Review individual and team sales performance metrics to identify top performers, consistent performers, and underperformers. Analyze factors such as sales revenue, conversion rates, average deal size, and sales cycle length. Identify patterns and trends to understand the strengths and weaknesses of your team. Example: John consistently exceeds his sales targets and has the highest conversion rate in the team, while

Sarah struggles to meet her quotas and has a low closing rate.

2. Skill Analysis: Assess the skills and competencies of your sales team members. Identify the specific skills required for success in your industry and sales process, such as prospecting, negotiation, relationship-building, product knowledge, and closing techniques. Compare the skill sets of your team members to determine areas of strength and areas that need improvement. Example: Mark is highly skilled in consultative selling and has excellent relationship-building abilities, whereas Lisa lacks proficiency in objection handling and needs further training in that area.

3. Knowledge and Expertise: Evaluate the product knowledge and industry expertise of your sales team. Determine if they possess a deep understanding of your products or services, as well as the industry landscape, market trends, and competitive landscape. Assess whether any knowledge gaps exist that could hinder their effectiveness in selling. Example: Mike demonstrates a comprehensive understanding of the product features, benefits, and competitive advantages, while Emily needs additional training to enhance her industry knowledge.

4. Team Dynamics: Evaluate the collaboration, communication, and teamwork within your sales team. Assess how well team members work together, share information, and support each other. Consider the team's overall morale, motivation, and willingness to cooperate. Example: The team exhibits strong

collaboration during weekly sales meetings, actively sharing best practices and offering support to each other, fostering a positive team dynamic.

5. Leadership Evaluation: Assess the effectiveness of sales leadership in guiding and developing the sales team. Evaluate the leadership style, communication, coaching, and mentoring provided to team members. Determine if there are areas where leadership could be improved to better support the sales team's success. Example: The sales manager consistently provides clear guidance, constructive feedback, and professional development opportunities, resulting in a motivated and high-performing sales team.

Using the Assessment to Define Your Hiring Strategy: Once you have conducted a comprehensive assessment of your current sales team, use the findings to define your sales hiring strategy. Consider the following approaches:

1. Addressing Skill Gaps: Identify specific skill gaps within your team and prioritize hiring individuals who possess those skills. For example, if your team lacks expertise in social selling, prioritize candidates who have a proven track record in leveraging social media for sales success.

2. Enhancing Product Knowledge: If your team lacks in-depth product knowledge, focus on hiring individuals who have experience in your industry or are quick learners with a strong desire to understand your products or services. Look for candidates who

demonstrate a genuine interest and curiosity in your offerings.

3. Balancing Strengths and Weaknesses: Use the assessment to create a well-rounded sales team by hiring individuals who complement the existing strengths and mitigate the weaknesses of your current team. For instance, if your team excels in relationship-building but lacks prospecting skills, prioritize candidates who have a strong background in lead generation.

4. Fostering Collaboration: Assess the team dynamics and identify opportunities to enhance collaboration and teamwork. Consider hiring individuals who have a track record of being team players and can contribute positively to the overall sales team culture.

Assessing your current sales team is a critical step in defining your sales hiring strategy. By evaluating the team's performance, skills, knowledge, team dynamics, and leadership, you can identify areas for improvement and align your hiring efforts to address those gaps. This assessment ensures that your hiring strategy is strategic, targeted, and focused on creating a high-performing sales team that can drive revenue growth and achieve organizational success.

Importance of Assessing the Current Sales Team, before Embarking on Hiring more Sales Professionals

Assessing the current sales team before hiring more sales professionals is important for several reasons:

1. Identify Strengths and Weaknesses: Assessing the current sales team allows you

to understand the strengths and weaknesses of the existing team members. This evaluation helps you determine areas where the team is excelling and areas where improvement is needed. By identifying these strengths and weaknesses, you can strategically hire new sales professionals who possess the skills and expertise necessary to fill the gaps in the team's capabilities.

2. Optimize Resource Allocation: Evaluating the current sales team helps you optimize resource allocation. You can determine if there is a need to redistribute workload or adjust territories based on the performance and skill sets of the current team members. This assessment ensures that you are leveraging the existing team's strengths and minimizing any potential overlaps or gaps in responsibilities before bringing in new hires.

3. Enhance Team Dynamics: Assessing the current sales team provides insights into team dynamics and collaboration. It helps you understand how team members interact, communicate, and work together. By identifying any issues or areas for improvement, you can address them before adding new members to the team. This ensures that the new hires will integrate smoothly into the existing team and contribute positively to a healthy and productive sales environment.

4. Define Hiring Needs: Evaluating the current sales team helps you define your hiring needs more accurately. By understanding the strengths and weaknesses of the team, you

can identify the specific skills, expertise, or experience that are lacking and need to be addressed through new hires. This assessment ensures that your hiring strategy is targeted and focused on finding candidates who can complement and enhance the existing team's capabilities.

5. Retain Top Performers: Assessing the current sales team allows you to identify and retain top performers. By recognizing the individuals who consistently achieve or exceed their targets, you can implement strategies to reward and retain them. This assessment helps you understand the factors that contribute to their success and create an environment that fosters their continued growth and motivation. Retaining top performers is crucial for maintaining a high-performing sales team and avoiding the potential negative impact of high turnover rates.

6. Strategic Hiring Decisions: Assessing the current sales team provides a foundation for making strategic hiring decisions. It helps you align your hiring strategy with the specific needs of the team and the organization's overall sales objectives. By understanding the strengths and weaknesses of the current team, you can prioritize hiring individuals who possess the skills and attributes necessary to drive sales growth, fill skill gaps, and enhance the team's overall performance.

Assessing the current sales team before hiring more sales professionals is essential for optimizing resource allocation, enhancing team dynamics, identifying hiring needs, retaining top performers, and making strategic hiring decisions. This evaluation ensures that the new hires complement the existing team, fill skill gaps, and contribute to the overall success of the sales organization.

Identifying Skill Gaps and Desired Competencies

To build a successful sales team, it is crucial to identify the skill gaps and desired competencies that will drive sales effectiveness and align with your organization's sales goals. This chapter focuses on the process of identifying skill gaps, determining the desired competencies, and provides examples to illustrate this process.

Identifying Skill Gaps: Identifying skill gaps involves assessing the current sales team's capabilities and comparing them to the skills required for success in your industry and sales environment. Here are some steps to help you identify skill gaps:

1. Review Sales Job Descriptions: Start by reviewing the job descriptions of your sales positions. Identify the core skills and competencies required for each role, such as prospecting, relationship-building, negotiation, closing, product knowledge, communication, and presentation skills. Example: A sales job description may require strong cold calling skills, the ability to build a robust pipeline, and excellent objection handling abilities.

2. Evaluate Current Team Skills: Assess the skills and competencies of your current sales team members. Determine if they possess the required skills outlined in the job descriptions. Evaluate their performance in various sales

activities and their proficiency in using sales tools and technologies. Example: After evaluating the team, you may find that some team members excel in relationship-building but lack strong closing skills or have limited experience with CRM software.

3. Analyze Sales Performance: Analyze sales performance metrics to identify areas where the team may be falling short. Look for patterns or trends that indicate specific skill gaps, such as consistently low conversion rates, difficulty in generating qualified leads, or challenges in overcoming objections. Example: If the team consistently struggles with objection handling and has a low closing rate, it indicates a skill gap in handling objections and closing deals effectively.

4. Seek Feedback: Gather feedback from sales managers, team members, and customers to gain insights into the team's strengths and weaknesses. Encourage open communication to understand which skills or competencies may be lacking or require improvement. Example: Feedback from sales managers may indicate that the team lacks advanced negotiation skills or that they need more training in consultative selling techniques.

Determining Desired Competencies: Once skill gaps have been identified, it is essential to determine the desired competencies that align with your organization's sales goals and values. Here's how you can determine the desired competencies:

1. Define Sales Objectives: Clearly define your sales objectives and the qualities that will contribute to achieving those goals. Consider

the specific sales strategies, market trends, and customer needs that are relevant to your organization. Example: If your sales objective is to increase market share by targeting enterprise-level clients, the desired competencies may include strategic thinking, relationship-building at the executive level, and the ability to navigate complex buying processes.

2. Align with Sales Methodology: Consider the sales methodology or approach used in your organization. Determine the competencies required to effectively implement that methodology, such as consultative selling, solution-oriented selling, or value-based selling. Example: If your organization follows a consultative selling approach, the desired competencies may include active listening, problem-solving, and the ability to ask probing questions to uncover customer needs.

3. Incorporate Industry Knowledge: Identify the specific industry knowledge or expertise that is valuable for your sales team. Consider the industry trends, competitive landscape, and product/service differentiation factors that impact the sales process. Example: If your organization operates in the technology industry, the desired competencies may include staying up-to-date with emerging technologies, understanding industry regulations, and articulating the value proposition in a technology-driven market.

4. Cultural Fit: Consider the cultural fit within your organization. Determine the competencies that align with your company

values, such as adaptability, resilience, teamwork, or customer-centricity. Example: If your organization values teamwork, the desired competencies may include collaboration, effective communication, and a willingness to support and learn from team members.

Identifying skill gaps and determining desired competencies is a crucial step in defining your sales hiring strategy. By understanding the skills your team currently lacks and the competencies required to achieve your sales goals, you can strategically hire sales professionals who possess those desired skills and attributes. This process ensures that you build a high-performing sales team capable of driving revenue growth, adapting to market changes, and consistently meeting customer needs.

Setting Clear Sales Objectives and Goals

Setting clear sales objectives and goals is a crucial step in defining your sales hiring strategy. This part focuses on the process of establishing sales objectives, the importance of aligning them with your organization's overall goals, and provides examples to illustrate this process.

The Importance of Setting Clear Sales Objectives: Clear sales objectives serve as a roadmap for your sales team, guiding their efforts and aligning them with your organization's broader goals. By setting specific and measurable objectives, you can create focus, motivation, and accountability within your sales team. Moreover, these objectives provide a benchmark for assessing the success of your sales hires and their contribution to your overall sales performance.

Steps for Setting Clear Sales Objectives and Goals:

1. Align with Organizational Goals: Start by aligning your sales objectives with your organization's overall goals. Consider the broader business objectives, such as revenue targets, market expansion, customer acquisition, or product penetration. Ensure that your sales objectives contribute directly to achieving these organizational goals. Example: If your organization's goal is to increase revenue by 20% in the next fiscal year, your sales objective may be to achieve a specific revenue target, such as a 30% increase in sales.

2. Identify Key Performance Indicators (KPIs): Determine the key performance indicators that will help you measure the success of your sales objectives. These metrics should be specific, measurable, attainable, relevant, and time-bound (SMART). Common sales KPIs include revenue, sales growth rate, customer acquisition rate, customer retention rate, and average deal size. Example: If your sales objective is to increase customer acquisition by 15%, the KPI could be measured by the number of new customers acquired within a specific time frame.

3. Break Down Objectives into Actionable Goals: Once you have defined your sales objectives, break them down into actionable goals that can be pursued by your sales team. These goals should be specific and clearly define what needs to be achieved, by whom, and within what timeframe. Example: If the sales

objective is to increase average deal size by 10%, an actionable goal could be for each sales representative to secure at least three up-sell or cross-sell opportunities per quarter.

4. Consider Sales Funnel Stages: Align your objectives and goals with different stages of the sales funnel. Consider objectives for lead generation, prospecting, closing deals, and post-sales activities such as customer retention and up-selling. This ensures a comprehensive approach to sales performance and allows you to identify specific areas where new hires can make a significant impact. Example: If your sales objective is to improve lead conversion rates, an actionable goal could be to increase the number of qualified leads generated by 20% within the first quarter.

5. Communicate Objectives to the Sales Team: Once your sales objectives and goals are defined, effectively communicate them to your sales team. Ensure that each team member understands their role in achieving these objectives and how their individual goals align with the broader sales strategy. Encourage transparency, collaboration, and accountability throughout the process. Example: Conduct a team meeting to communicate the sales objectives and goals, provide clarity on expectations, and allow team members to ask questions or provide input.

6. Monitor and Evaluate Progress: Regularly monitor and evaluate the progress towards your sales objectives and goals. Use sales analytics, performance dashboards, and

regular check-ins with your team to track key metrics and assess individual and team performance. Adjust goals or strategies as needed based on real-time insights and market dynamics. Example: Conduct weekly or monthly sales reviews to review individual and team progress, analyze performance metrics, and make data-driven adjustments to the sales strategy.

Setting clear sales objectives and goals is crucial for driving sales performance and aligning your sales hiring strategy with your organization's overall goals. By establishing specific and measurable objectives, breaking them down into actionable goals, and regularly monitoring progress, you create a framework for success and provide a clear direction for your sales team. This clarity helps guide your hiring decisions, ensuring that new sales professionals are aligned with your sales objectives and can contribute effectively to achieving them.

Establishing a Sales Hiring Budget

Establishing a sales hiring budget is a critical aspect of your sales hiring strategy. So here we will focus on the process of determining a budget for your sales hiring efforts and provide examples to illustrate this process.

The Importance of Establishing a Sales Hiring Budget: A well-defined sales hiring budget helps ensure that your recruitment efforts are strategic, efficient, and aligned with your organization's financial resources. It allows you to allocate funds appropriately, invest in effective recruitment channels, and attract top sales talent while managing costs. By establishing a sales hiring budget, you can make informed decisions about where to allocate your resources to maximize the return on investment in your sales hiring process.

Steps for Establishing a Sales Hiring Budget:

1. Assess Current Resources: Begin by assessing your organization's current financial resources and capabilities. Evaluate your budget constraints, financial projections, and the overall financial health of your company. This assessment will help you determine how much you can allocate towards sales hiring. Example: If your organization has a budget surplus and is experiencing steady growth, you may have more flexibility to allocate a larger budget for sales hiring efforts.

2. Determine Hiring Needs: Evaluate your sales hiring needs based on your sales objectives, team capacity, and growth projections. Consider factors such as anticipated turnover, expansion into new markets, or the launch of new products/services. This assessment will help you determine the volume and frequency of sales hires required. Example: If your sales objective is to penetrate a new market, you may need to hire a team of sales professionals to support that expansion.

3. Research Recruitment Costs: Research and gather information on recruitment costs associated with various channels, including job boards, recruitment agencies, social media advertising, career fairs, and employee referrals. Obtain quotes and estimates from different vendors or platforms to determine the costs involved. Example: Based on your research, you may find that a specialized

recruitment agency charges a fee equivalent to a percentage of the new hire's annual salary, while job board postings have a fixed cost per listing.

4. Consider Recruitment Methods: Evaluate the effectiveness and efficiency of different recruitment methods based on your organization's needs and budget. Consider the cost per hire, time-to-fill positions, and the quality of candidates sourced through each method. Assess which methods have yielded successful hires in the past and prioritize those. Example: You may find that employee referrals have resulted in high-quality hires at a lower cost compared to job board postings, indicating that allocating a portion of your budget to referral bonuses may be a cost-effective strategy.

5. Allocate Budget Components: Determine how to allocate your sales hiring budget across different components, such as recruitment advertising, candidate screening tools, background checks, travel expenses for interviews, recruitment agency fees, or employee referral incentives. Consider the relative importance of each component and allocate funds accordingly. Example: If you find that recruitment advertising has been a successful source of qualified candidates in the past, you may allocate a larger portion of your budget to job board postings or social media advertising.

6. Plan for Contingencies: Set aside a portion of your sales hiring budget for unexpected or additional costs that may arise during the

recruitment process. This allows for flexibility in case of unforeseen circumstances or the need to adjust the hiring strategy. Example: You may allocate a small percentage of your budget as a contingency fund to cover potential additional recruitment agency fees or travel expenses for out-of-state candidates.

Establishing a sales hiring budget is crucial for effective resource allocation, cost management, and attracting top sales talent. By assessing your financial resources, understanding your hiring needs, researching recruitment costs, considering different recruitment methods, and planning for contingencies, you can create a well-defined budget that supports your sales hiring strategy. This ensures that you can efficiently invest in recruitment efforts, maximize the quality of your hires, and achieve your sales objectives within your financial constraints.

Chapter 3
Creating Effective
Sales Job Descriptions

Creating Effective Sales Job Descriptions

Understanding the Role and Responsibilities
Creating effective sales job descriptions is essential for attracting qualified candidates and ensuring a strong fit between the role and the candidates' skills and experience. This chapter focuses on understanding the role and responsibilities of sales positions and provides examples to illustrate this process.

Understanding the Role: To create an effective sales job description, it is crucial to have a clear understanding of the role within your organization. Consider the following steps to gain a comprehensive understanding of the sales role:

1. Analyze Sales Functions: Identify the specific functions and activities that the sales role entails within your organization. Sales functions may include prospecting, lead generation, relationship-building, negotiation, closing deals, account management, or post-sales support. Understand the primary focus and priorities of the role. Example: In a B2B sales role, the focus may be on building and nurturing long-term client relationships, whereas in a B2C sales role, the emphasis may be on generating a high volume of sales through direct customer interactions.

2. Assess Target Market and Customers: Determine the target market and customer segments that the sales role will be responsible for. Understand the characteristics of these target customers, their needs, pain

points, and purchasing behaviors. This understanding will help tailor the job description to attract candidates with relevant industry experience or customer knowledge. Example: If the target market is the healthcare industry, the sales role may require knowledge of healthcare regulations, understanding of medical products, and experience in selling to healthcare professionals.

3. Consider Sales Cycle Length: Assess the length of the sales cycle and the typical duration from prospecting to closing deals. Understand whether the sales role requires long-term relationship-building or involves shorter, transactional sales cycles. This knowledge will help set appropriate expectations for the role. Example: In enterprise sales, where the sales cycle may span several months or even years, the sales role may require strong relationship-building skills and the ability to navigate complex decision-making processes.

Understanding Responsibilities: Once you have a clear understanding of the sales role, it is essential to define the specific responsibilities and tasks that the sales professional will be accountable for. Consider the following steps to outline the responsibilities:

1. Define Core Responsibilities: Identify the key responsibilities that the sales professional will be responsible for in their day-to-day activities. These may include tasks such as prospecting new leads, conducting sales presentations, negotiating contracts, managing accounts, or achieving sales targets. Example: Core responsibilities for a sales role may include

conducting product demonstrations, identifying up-sell opportunities, and achieving monthly revenue targets.

2. Prioritize Responsibilities: Prioritize the responsibilities based on their importance and impact on sales success. Highlight the key responsibilities that will significantly contribute to achieving sales goals and the overall success of the sales team. Example: If building a strong pipeline is crucial for sales success, emphasize the responsibility of prospecting and lead generation in the job description.

3. Determine Reporting Relationships: Specify the reporting relationships within the organization. Clarify who the sales professional will report to, who they will collaborate with, and any supervisory responsibilities they may have. Example: The sales professional may report to a Sales Manager and collaborate with cross-functional teams such as marketing, customer support, or product development.

4. Outline Performance Expectations: Clearly define the performance expectations for the role, including sales targets, key performance indicators (KPIs), and any specific metrics used to evaluate success. This helps candidates understand the expectations and motivates them to perform at a high level. Example: The job description may specify that the sales professional is expected to achieve a monthly revenue target of $X, maintain a conversion rate of X%, and generate X number of qualified leads per month.

5. Include Growth Opportunities: Highlight any potential growth opportunities or career progression paths available within the organization. This can attract ambitious candidates who are seeking long-term career development. Example: Mention that the sales role offers opportunities for advancement into sales management or the potential to specialize in a particular industry or product line.

Understanding the role and responsibilities is a crucial first step in creating effective sales job descriptions. By analyzing sales functions, assessing the target market and customers, considering the sales cycle length, defining core responsibilities, prioritizing them, determining reporting relationships, outlining performance expectations, and including growth opportunities, you can create job descriptions that accurately reflect the role and attract qualified candidates who are a strong fit for your sales team.

Defining Sales Targets and Quotas

Defining sales targets and quotas is a crucial aspect of creating effective sales job descriptions. This section focuses on understanding the importance of setting clear targets and quotas, and provides examples to illustrate this process.

The Importance of Defining Sales Targets and Quotas: Sales targets and quotas provide a clear benchmark for sales professionals to work towards. They serve as performance indicators and align the efforts of the sales team with the organization's revenue objectives. Clearly defined targets and quotas motivate sales professionals, create accountability, and enable the measurement of individual and team performance.

Steps for Defining Sales Targets and Quotas:

1. Set Realistic Sales Targets: Start by setting realistic sales targets based on historical data, market trends, and organizational goals. Consider factors such as industry growth rates, market share, competition, and product/service offerings. It is essential to strike a balance between setting challenging targets and ensuring they are attainable. Example: If the company experienced 10% revenue growth last year, setting a target of 20% growth for the upcoming year may be realistic and challenging.

2. Break Down Targets by Timeframe: Divide the sales targets into specific timeframes to provide a clear roadmap for sales professionals. Common timeframes include monthly, quarterly, and annual targets. Breaking down targets allows for better tracking of progress and enables timely adjustments to strategies if necessary. Example: If the annual sales target is $1 million, break it down into monthly targets of approximately $83,333 to guide sales activities.

3. Consider Individual and Team Quotas: Determine whether individual quotas, team quotas, or a combination of both will be used. Individual quotas focus on individual sales professionals' performance, while team quotas foster collaboration and encourage teamwork. Consider the sales role and the organization's culture when deciding which approach to

adopt. Example: In a competitive environment, individual quotas may be more suitable, while in a collaborative sales culture, team quotas can promote a sense of collective achievement.

4. Align Quotas with Sales Roles: Tailor quotas to align with the specific responsibilities and objectives of each sales role. Different sales roles may have distinct metrics and targets based on their position in the sales cycle, customer segmentation, or product focus. Ensure that quotas reflect the unique contribution of each sales role to the overall sales process. Example: For an account manager responsible for managing and up-selling existing accounts, the quota may be based on the percentage increase in revenue from those accounts.

5. Make Quotas Measurable and Trackable: Ensure that quotas are measurable and trackable to monitor individual and team performance accurately. Define specific metrics or Key Performance Indicators (KPIs) associated with each quota to provide clarity and enable performance evaluation. Example: If the quota is based on revenue, track the sales professional's progress by monitoring their actual sales revenue against the assigned quota.

6. Provide Incentives and Rewards: Consider incorporating incentive plans or rewards tied to achieving sales targets and quotas. Incentives can motivate sales professionals to exceed expectations and create a sense of recognition and reward for exceptional

performance. Example: Offer bonuses, commissions, or recognition programs for surpassing individual or team quotas, such as a monthly bonus for achieving 110% of the monthly sales target.

Defining sales targets and quotas is essential for creating effective sales job descriptions. By setting realistic targets, breaking them down into timeframes, considering individual and team quotas, aligning quotas with sales roles, making them measurable and trackable, and providing incentives and rewards, you can create job descriptions that clearly outline the performance expectations for sales professionals. This not only motivates them but also enables effective performance measurement and contributes to the overall success of your sales team.

Outlining Key Skills and Qualifications

Outlining key skills and qualifications in sales job descriptions is vital for attracting qualified candidates who possess the necessary attributes to excel in the role. This chapter focuses on understanding the importance of identifying key skills and qualifications, and provides examples to illustrate this process.

The Importance of Outlining Key Skills and Qualifications: Clearly defining the required skills and qualifications in sales job descriptions ensures that you attract candidates who have the essential capabilities to succeed in the role. It helps set expectations for potential applicants and allows them to assess their fit for the position. Outlining these requirements also streamlines the candidate screening process by allowing you to quickly identify candidates who meet the necessary criteria.

Steps for Outlining Key Skills and Qualifications:

1. Identify Essential Sales Skills: Begin by identifying the essential sales skills that are critical for success in the role. Consider the specific requirements of the sales position, such as prospecting, relationship-building, negotiation, presentation, closing, or account management. Determine which skills are essential and which ones are desirable but not mandatory. Example: Essential sales skills may include excellent communication and interpersonal skills, strong persuasion abilities, and a track record of meeting or exceeding sales targets.
2. Determine Product or Industry Knowledge: Assess whether specific product knowledge or industry experience is required for the sales role. Depending on the complexity of the product/service being sold or the industry in which it operates, candidates may need to demonstrate a level of familiarity or expertise. Example: If you're hiring for a medical device sales role, it may be necessary for candidates to possess knowledge of medical terminology, regulations, and an understanding of healthcare providers' needs.
3. Specify Educational Background: Determine the educational background or academic qualifications that are relevant to the sales position. Consider whether a specific degree, certification, or specialized training is necessary or preferred for the role. Example: For a technical sales role, a degree in engineering or a related field may be desirable to understand complex technical concepts and effectively communicate with customers.

4. Highlight Relevant Experience: Outline the required level of sales experience for the position. Consider the desired number of years of experience, specific types of sales experience (B2B, B2C, inside sales, field sales), and any industry-specific experience that would be valuable. Example: If you're hiring for a senior sales position, you may require a minimum of 5 years of experience in a similar sales role, preferably in the same industry.

5. Emphasize Personal Traits and Attributes: Identify personal traits and attributes that are important for success in the sales role. These can include characteristics such as resilience, self-motivation, adaptability, and a results-oriented mindset. Example: In a high-pressure sales environment, emphasizing the need for resilience and the ability to handle rejection can help attract candidates who thrive in such situations.

6. Prioritize Skills and Qualifications: Prioritize the outlined skills and qualifications based on their importance for the role. Differentiate between must-have requirements and those that are preferred but not essential. This helps candidates understand the critical skills needed for the position. Example: If strong communication skills are critical for the role, make it a must-have requirement, while proficiency in a specific software program may be listed as a preferred qualification.

Outlining key skills and qualifications in sales job descriptions is crucial for attracting qualified candidates and streamlining the candidate screening process. By identifying essential sales skills, determining product or industry knowledge, specifying educational background, highlighting relevant experience, emphasizing personal traits, and prioritizing the requirements, you can create job descriptions that clearly communicate the skills and qualifications necessary for success in the sales role. This ensures that you attract candidates who possess the desired attributes and increases the likelihood of finding the right fit for your sales team.

Crafting Compelling Job Descriptions

Crafting compelling job descriptions is essential for attracting top sales talent. A well-written job description not only communicates the role's responsibilities and requirements but also captures the attention and interest of potential candidates. This chapter focuses on the importance of crafting compelling job descriptions and provides examples to illustrate this process.

The Importance of Crafting Compelling Job Descriptions: A compelling job description serves as a powerful tool to attract qualified candidates and differentiate your company from competitors. It provides potential applicants with a clear understanding of the role, its challenges, and the opportunities it offers. A well-crafted job description can generate excitement, engage candidates, and encourage them to apply.

Steps for Crafting Compelling Job Descriptions:

1. Start with an Engaging Introduction: Begin the job description with a captivating introduction that highlights the company's culture, values, and mission. Use this section to create a positive first impression and capture the

candidate's attention. Example: "Join our dynamic and innovative team at XYZ Company, where we are revolutionizing the industry with cutting-edge solutions. If you are a highly motivated and results-driven sales professional, we invite you to be a part of our success story."

2. Clearly Outline the Job Title and Role: Clearly state the job title and provide a concise overview of the role's responsibilities and objectives. This helps candidates quickly understand the nature of the position and its relevance to their skills and career aspirations. Example: "Sales Executive - Responsibilities include driving new business acquisition, nurturing client relationships, and achieving sales targets within the assigned territory."

3. Highlight Key Responsibilities: Provide a detailed description of the role's key responsibilities, focusing on the most important and impactful tasks. Clearly communicate the day-to-day activities, highlighting the challenges and opportunities the role presents. Example: "Generate leads through proactive prospecting and networking efforts. Conduct sales presentations and product demonstrations to educate potential clients on the value of our solutions. Develop and maintain strong relationships with key decision-makers. Negotiate contracts and close deals, ensuring customer satisfaction throughout the sales process."

4. Describe Desired Skills and Qualifications: Outline the required skills, qualifications, and experience necessary for success in the role.

Be specific about the desired attributes, industry knowledge, technical proficiencies, and soft skills needed to excel. Example: "Bachelor's degree in Business Administration or a related field. Minimum of 3 years of experience in B2B sales, with a proven track record of meeting or exceeding sales targets. Strong communication and interpersonal skills, with the ability to build rapport and influence decision-makers. Experience in the software industry and familiarity with CRM systems preferred."

5. Showcase Benefits and Perks: Highlight the benefits, perks, and unique aspects of working for your company. Emphasize career development opportunities, competitive compensation packages, incentive plans, flexible work arrangements, and any other attractive benefits. Example: "We offer a competitive base salary with an uncapped commission structure, allowing you to earn unlimited income. Comprehensive health and wellness benefits, including medical, dental, and vision coverage. Ongoing training and development programs to enhance your sales skills and career progression. Flexible work hours and the opportunity for remote work."

6. Use a Compelling Tone and Language: Use a conversational and persuasive tone throughout the job description. Engage candidates by focusing on the positive aspects of the role and the company culture. Avoid jargon and complex language, making the description easily understandable and relatable. Example: "We are seeking

ambitious sales professionals who thrive in a fast-paced environment and are passionate about delivering exceptional results. If you are a natural relationship builder with a hunger for success, this is the opportunity you've been waiting for."

Crafting compelling job descriptions is vital for attracting top sales talent. By starting with an engaging introduction, clearly outlining the job title and role, highlighting key responsibilities, describing desired skills and qualifications, showcasing benefits and perks, and using a compelling tone and language, you can create job descriptions that capture the interest of potential candidates and motivate them to apply. Remember, a well-crafted job description sets the foundation for finding the right sales professionals who will contribute to the success of your organization.

Sample Sales Job Descriptions

Sample Sales Job Description 1: Sales Representative

Company: XYZ Corporation Location: Any-town, New Country

Job Description: XYZ Corporation is seeking a highly motivated and results-driven Sales Representative to join our sales team. As a Sales Representative, you will be responsible for generating new business opportunities, building relationships with clients, and driving sales revenue.

Responsibilities:

1. Prospect and generate leads through various channels such as cold calling, networking, and referrals.

2. Conduct product demonstrations and presentations to potential clients.
3. Build and maintain strong relationships with existing clients to ensure customer satisfaction and loyalty.
4. Collaborate with the sales team to develop sales strategies and achieve sales targets.
5. Stay updated on industry trends, market conditions, and competitor activities.
6. Prepare and deliver sales proposals, contracts, and pricing negotiations.
7. Provide timely and accurate sales reports to the sales manager.

Requirements:
1. Proven track record of achieving sales targets and driving revenue growth.
2. Excellent communication and interpersonal skills.
3. Strong negotiation and closing skills.
4. Ability to work independently and in a team environment.
5. Knowledge of the industry and understanding of customer needs.
6. Proficiency in CRM software and sales tools.
7. Bachelor's degree in Business, Marketing, or a related field.

Sample Sales Job Description 2: Account Manager

Company: ABC Solutions Location: City, State, Country

Job Description: ABC Solutions is seeking a dynamic and client-focused Account Manager to join our team. As an Account Manager, you will be responsible for managing and growing a portfolio of key accounts, building strong relationships, and driving customer satisfaction.

Responsibilities:
1. Manage a portfolio of existing accounts and foster long-term relationships with key stakeholders.
2. Understand client needs and develop tailored solutions to meet their objectives.
3. Conduct regular business reviews and identify opportunities for up-selling and cross-selling.
4. Collaborate with internal teams to ensure seamless delivery of products and services.
5. Address client concerns, resolve issues, and ensure high levels of customer satisfaction.
6. Stay updated on industry trends and market dynamics to identify growth opportunities.
7. Prepare sales reports, forecasts, and presentations for management.

Requirements:
1. Proven experience as an Account Manager or in a similar client-facing role.
2. Strong relationship-building and interpersonal skills.
3. Excellent communication and presentation skills.
4. Ability to manage multiple accounts and prioritize tasks effectively.
5. Results-oriented mindset with a focus on exceeding targets.
6. Knowledge of the industry and understanding of client needs.
7. Bachelor's degree in Business, Marketing, or a related field.

**Sample Sales Job Description
3: Sales Manager**

Company: XYZ Solutions Location: Any-town, New Country

Job Description: XYZ Solutions is seeking an experienced and strategic Sales Manager to lead our sales team. As a Sales Manager, you will be responsible for driving sales performance, developing sales strategies, and managing the sales team to achieve targets.

Responsibilities:

1. Develop and execute sales strategies to meet or exceed revenue targets.
2. Manage and coach a team of sales representatives to drive performance and achieve sales goals.
3. Set clear sales targets and monitor team progress towards those targets.
4. Identify market opportunities, analyze competitors, and develop sales plans to capitalize on opportunities.
5. Build and maintain strong relationships with key clients and stakeholders.
6. Conduct regular sales meetings and provide guidance, support, and feedback to the sales team.
7. Prepare and present sales forecasts, reports, and analysis to senior management.

Requirements:

1. Proven experience as a Sales Manager or in a similar sales leadership role.
2. Strong leadership and team management skills.
3. Excellent communication and negotiation skills.

4. Strategic thinking and ability to develop and implement sales strategies.
5. Results-oriented mindset with a track record of achieving sales targets.
6. Knowledge of the industry and understanding of market dynamics.
7. Bachelor's degree in Business, Marketing, or a related field.

Sample Sales Job Description 4: Inside Sales Representative

Company: ABC Tech Solutions Location: City, State, Country

Job Description: ABC Tech Solutions is seeking a motivated and proactive Inside Sales Representative to join our sales team. As an Inside Sales Representative, you will be responsible for prospecting, qualifying leads, and converting them into customers through phone and email communications.

Responsibilities:
1. Prospect and generate leads through outbound calls and email campaigns.
2. Qualify leads by understanding their needs and assessing their fit for our products.
3. Conduct product presentations and demonstrations to potential customers.
4. Manage and update customer information in the CRM system.
5. Collaborate with the sales team to meet and exceed sales targets.
6. Provide excellent customer service and address customer inquiries and concerns.
7. Stay updated on industry trends and product knowledge.

Requirements:
1. Proven experience in inside sales or telemarketing.
2. Strong communication and interpersonal skills.
3. Self-motivated and target-driven mindset.
4. Ability to work independently and in a team environment.
5. Proficient in using CRM software and sales tools.
6. Knowledge of the industry and understanding of customer needs.
7. High school diploma or equivalent; Bachelor's degree is a plus.

Sample Sales Job Description 5: Territory Sales Manager

Company: XYZ Manufacturing Location: Any-town, New Country

Job Description: XYZ Manufacturing is seeking a Territory Sales Manager to oversee sales activities in a designated geographic region. As a Territory Sales Manager, you will be responsible for driving revenue growth, building relationships with distributors, and managing sales operations in your assigned territory.

Responsibilities:
1. Develop and execute sales plans to achieve revenue targets in the assigned territory.
2. Identify and pursue new business opportunities by prospecting and engaging with potential customers.
3. Build and maintain strong relationships with distributors and key stakeholders.
4. Conduct product training sessions for distributors and their sales teams.

5. Monitor market trends, competitor activities, and customer needs.
6. Provide sales forecasts, reports, and analysis to management.
7. Collaborate with internal teams to ensure timely order fulfillment and customer satisfaction.

Requirements:

1. Proven experience as a Territory Sales Manager or in a similar role.
2. Strong sales and negotiation skills.
3. Ability to build and maintain relationships with distributors and customers.
4. Excellent communication and presentation skills.
5. Analytical and strategic thinking.
6. Knowledge of the industry and understanding of market dynamics.
7. Bachelor's degree in Business, Marketing, or a related field.

These sample sales job descriptions provide an overview of the typical responsibilities and requirements for various sales positions. Employers can customize these descriptions to align with their specific needs and industry requirements.

Chapter 4
Sourcing Sales Candidates

Sourcing Sales Candidates

Traditional Methods of Sourcing Sales Talent

Sourcing sales candidates is a critical step in finding top sales talent for your organization. In this chapter, we will explore traditional methods of sourcing sales talent. These methods have been widely used and proven effective in attracting qualified candidates.

Traditional Methods of Sourcing Sales Talent:

1. Job Boards and Online Job Postings: Job boards and online job postings are popular platforms for sourcing sales talent. These platforms allow you to reach a wide audience of potential candidates actively searching for sales opportunities. You can post detailed job descriptions and qualifications, and applicants can easily submit their resumes and cover letters. Example: Utilize popular job boards like Indeed, LinkedIn, or industry-specific job portals to advertise your sales positions.

2. Referrals: Leveraging employee referrals is a valuable way to source sales candidates. Current employees can refer individuals from their network who they believe are qualified for the sales role. Referrals often result in high-quality candidates who are a good fit for the company culture. Example: Implement an employee referral program that incentivizes employees to refer qualified sales candidates. Offer rewards, such as bonuses or recognition, for successful referrals that result in a hire.

3. Networking Events: Attending networking events, trade shows, conferences, and industry-specific gatherings provides opportunities to meet sales professionals face-to-face. These events allow you to establish connections, engage in conversations, and identify potential candidates who are actively involved in the sales community. Example: Participate in industry conferences and engage with attendees to identify sales professionals who exhibit strong industry knowledge and networking skills.

4. Professional Associations: Professional associations dedicated to sales or specific industries often have resources for sourcing sales talent. These associations provide access to a pool of sales professionals who are committed to professional development and networking within their respective fields. Example: Research and join professional associations related to sales, such as the National Association of Sales Professionals (NASP), and utilize their member directories or job boards to find qualified sales candidates.

5. Print Advertisements: Though less common in the digital age, print advertisements in industry publications, newspapers, or trade magazines can still be effective for sourcing sales talent. These advertisements can reach a targeted audience and capture the attention of professionals actively seeking sales opportunities. Example: Place a print advertisement in a trade magazine specific to

your industry to attract experienced sales professionals with domain knowledge.

6. Recruitment Agencies: Working with recruitment agencies specializing in sales can be an efficient way to source qualified sales candidates. These agencies have a network of pre-screened sales professionals and can assist in finding candidates who match your specific requirements. Example: Engage with sales-focused recruitment agencies that understand your industry and the specific sales roles you are hiring for.

Traditional methods of sourcing sales talent provide a solid foundation for finding qualified candidates. By utilizing job boards and online postings, leveraging employee referrals, attending networking events, tapping into professional associations, utilizing print advertisements, and collaborating with recruitment agencies, you can attract a diverse pool of sales professionals who align with your organization's needs and contribute to its success. Keep in mind that combining traditional methods with modern approaches can further enhance your ability to find top sales talent.

Leveraging Online Job Boards and Career Platforms

In today's digital age, online job boards and career platforms have become a prominent method for sourcing sales candidates. This chapter focuses on leveraging these platforms to attract top sales talent. We will explore the benefits of using online job boards and career platforms and provide examples to illustrate their effectiveness.

Benefits of Leveraging Online Job Boards and Career Platforms:

1. Wide Reach and Visibility: Online job boards and career platforms offer a vast reach, allowing you to connect with a large pool of potential candidates. These platforms attract job seekers actively searching for sales opportunities and provide a platform for you to showcase your company and available positions. Example: Utilize popular job boards like Indeed, LinkedIn, Glassdoor, or Monster to access a wide audience of sales professionals actively seeking new career opportunities.

2. Targeted Candidate Search: Online job boards and career platforms allow you to target specific candidate criteria based on job title, industry, location, experience level, and desired skills. This feature helps you narrow down the candidate pool and focus on individuals who closely match your requirements. Example: Utilize advanced search filters on job boards to target candidates with specific sales experience, such as B2B sales, enterprise sales, or retail sales.

3. Access to Active Job Seekers: These platforms attract active job seekers who actively browse and apply to job postings. This increases the likelihood of connecting with candidates who are actively seeking sales opportunities and are motivated to make a career move. Example: Utilize the job alert feature on job boards to notify candidates when a new sales position matching their

criteria is posted, keeping them engaged and informed.

4. Employer Branding and Company Profile: Online job boards and career platforms allow you to showcase your company's brand and culture through employer branding features. You can create a compelling company profile that highlights your unique selling points, values, and work environment. This helps attract candidates who align with your company's values and vision. Example: Utilize the company profile section on LinkedIn or Glassdoor to showcase your company culture, mission, and employee testimonials, creating a compelling brand presence.

5. Application Management and Screening Tools: Online job boards and career platforms provide tools for managing applications, including applicant tracking systems (ATS) and screening features. These tools streamline the candidate selection process, making it easier to review resumes, track candidate interactions, and identify the most promising candidates. Example: Utilize the built-in ATS features on job boards to track candidate progress, collaborate with hiring team members, and maintain a centralized database of applicant information.

6. Candidate Engagement and Communication: Online platforms facilitate seamless communication with candidates throughout the hiring process. You can easily connect with applicants, schedule interviews, and provide updates on the hiring status. This improves candidate experience and demonstrates your

commitment to effective communication. Example: Utilize messaging features on job boards and career platforms to engage with candidates, answer their queries, and provide timely updates.

Leveraging online job boards and career platforms provides numerous advantages for sourcing top sales talent. By utilizing their wide reach, targeted candidate search capabilities, access to active job seekers, employer branding features, application management tools, and effective candidate communication, you can attract qualified sales professionals who align with your company's needs and culture. Remember to optimize your job postings with compelling descriptions and relevant keywords to increase visibility and attract the best sales candidates.

Utilizing Social Media for Sales Recruitment

Social media has become a powerful tool for sourcing sales candidates. In this chapter, we will explore the benefits of utilizing social media platforms for sales recruitment. We will discuss the different social media platforms suitable for sourcing sales talent and provide examples to illustrate their effectiveness.

Benefits of Utilizing Social Media for Sales Recruitment:

1. Wide Reach and Targeted Audience: Social media platforms, such as LinkedIn, Facebook, Twitter, and Instagram, have billions of active users worldwide. These platforms allow you to reach a wide audience and target specific demographics and professional backgrounds.

This provides an opportunity to connect with sales professionals who may not actively be searching for a job but are open to new opportunities. Example: Utilize LinkedIn, a professional networking platform, to target sales professionals based on their industry, job title, skills, and experience.

2. Showcasing Company Culture and Employer Brand: Social media platforms offer an avenue to showcase your company culture, values, and employer brand. By posting engaging content that reflects your company's values, achievements, and work environment, you can attract sales candidates who resonate with your brand and vision. Example: Share employee testimonials, behind-the-scenes photos, and videos that highlight your company culture and the success stories of your sales team.

3. Building a Talent Pipeline: Social media platforms allow you to build a talent pipeline by creating connections and engaging with potential sales candidates. You can develop relationships with passive candidates and nurture them over time, ensuring a pool of qualified candidates when a sales position becomes available. Example: Engage with sales professionals on LinkedIn by sharing industry insights, participating in relevant groups, and commenting on their posts to establish connections and stay on their radar.

4. Employee Advocacy and Referrals: Leveraging your employees as brand advocates on social media can significantly expand your reach and attract sales talent.

Encourage employees to share job openings and company updates with their networks, increasing the likelihood of reaching qualified candidates through referrals. Example: Implement an employee advocacy program where employees are encouraged to share job postings on their personal social media profiles and provide incentives for successful referrals.

5. Engaging with Sales Communities and Groups: Social media platforms offer numerous sales communities, groups, and forums where professionals discuss industry trends, challenges, and opportunities. Engaging with these communities allows you to connect with active sales professionals, establish your presence as a thought leader, and identify potential candidates. Example: Participate in sales-focused LinkedIn groups or Twitter chats related to your industry and actively contribute to discussions, demonstrating your expertise and creating opportunities for candidate engagement.

6. Utilizing Paid Advertising and Sponsored Content: Social media platforms offer paid advertising and sponsored content options that allow you to boost the visibility of your job postings and reach a targeted audience of sales professionals. These features enable you to optimize your recruitment campaigns and ensure your job openings are seen by relevant candidates. Example: Utilize LinkedIn's sponsored job postings or Facebook's targeted advertising options to

reach a specific demographic of sales professionals in your desired location.

Utilizing social media for sales recruitment offers numerous benefits, including wide reach, targeted audience, showcasing company culture, building a talent pipeline, employee advocacy, engaging with sales communities, and utilizing paid advertising. By incorporating social media platforms into your recruitment strategy, you can attract top sales talent, establish your brand presence, and create connections with potential candidates. Remember to maintain an active and engaging presence, share valuable content, and leverage your employees as brand advocates to maximize the effectiveness of social media for sales recruitment.

Networking and Referrals for Finding Top Sales Professionals

Networking and referrals are powerful methods for sourcing top sales professionals. This chapter focuses on utilizing networking events and leveraging employee referrals to find highly qualified sales candidates. We will explore the benefits of networking and referrals and provide examples to illustrate their effectiveness.

Benefits of Networking and Referrals for Finding Top Sales Professionals:

1. Access to Hidden Talent: Networking events and referrals provide access to a hidden pool of talented sales professionals who may not be actively searching for job opportunities. These individuals are often highly skilled and experienced, making them valuable assets for your organization. Example: Attend industry conferences, trade shows, and sales-focused

networking events to connect with sales professionals who are actively engaged in the industry.

2. Trust and Credibility: When you receive a referral from a trusted source, such as an employee or professional connection, it carries a higher level of trust and credibility. Referrals often result in high-quality candidates who have already been vetted to some extent by the referrer. Example: Establish an employee referral program that incentivizes employees to refer qualified sales candidates. Encourage employees to tap into their networks, such as former colleagues, industry peers, or sales contacts, to find potential candidates.

3. Cultural Fit: Referrals tend to align with the company culture more closely since the referrer understands the organization's values and work environment. This increases the likelihood of finding candidates who will seamlessly integrate into the sales team and contribute to its success. Example: Encourage employees to refer individuals who not only possess the required sales skills but also exhibit cultural fit and share the company's values and vision.

4. Cost and Time Efficiency: Networking and referrals can save significant time and resources in the recruitment process. Since referrals often result in a higher quality candidate pool, you can reduce the time and effort spent on sourcing and screening candidates. Example: Maintain a strong network of industry contacts, engage with professionals on social media platforms, and

encourage employees to actively participate in industry events to expand your referral network.

5. Expanded Reach: Networking events provide opportunities to connect with professionals from various industries, organizations, and backgrounds. This expands your reach beyond traditional recruitment channels and allows you to tap into diverse talent pools. Example: Attend local business association events, join sales-focused networking groups, and participate in online forums and communities to broaden your network and connect with a wider range of sales professionals.

6. Ongoing Relationship Building: Networking and referrals offer the potential for ongoing relationship building with sales professionals. Even if a referral does not result in an immediate hire, maintaining connections and nurturing relationships can lead to future opportunities for collaboration or future job openings. Example: Stay in touch with promising candidates who may not be the right fit for the current role but could be a valuable asset in the future. Engage with them through occasional follow-ups, industry updates, or professional development opportunities.

Networking and referrals are valuable strategies for sourcing top sales professionals. By attending networking events, engaging with industry professionals, establishing employee referral programs, and nurturing relationships, you can tap into hidden talent, benefit from trusted recommendations, find candidates who align with your company culture, save time and resources, expand your reach, and build ongoing connections. Incorporate networking and referrals into your sales recruitment strategy to access a pool of highly qualified sales professionals and enhance the success of your hiring efforts.

Chapter 5
Assessing
Sales Candidates

Assessing Sales Candidates

The Importance of a Structured Interview Process

The assessment of sales candidates is a crucial step in the hiring process to ensure you select the most qualified individuals for your sales team. In this chapter, we will explore the importance of implementing a structured interview process and its benefits. We will provide examples and guidelines to help you create an effective and fair interview process.

The Importance of a Structured Interview Process:

1. Consistency and Fairness: A structured interview process ensures consistency and fairness in evaluating candidates. It provides a standardized approach where all candidates are assessed using the same set of criteria, allowing for a fair comparison of their skills, experience, and qualifications. Example: Develop a list of standardized interview questions that assess key competencies required for the sales role, such as communication skills, negotiation abilities, and relationship-building capabilities. Ask these questions to all candidates to ensure a fair evaluation.

2. Valid and Reliable Assessment: A structured interview process enhances the validity and reliability of candidate assessment. By using predetermined questions and evaluation criteria, you can better predict a candidate's potential for success in the sales role and

make more informed hiring decisions. Example: Use behavioral-based interview questions that require candidates to provide specific examples of past sales experiences, demonstrating their abilities in real-life scenarios. This approach provides insights into how candidates have applied their skills and achieved results.

3. Identification of Key Competencies: A structured interview process allows you to identify and assess the key competencies required for success in the sales role. By aligning interview questions with the desired skills and traits, you can evaluate candidates based on their ability to meet these requirements. Example: If a critical competency for the sales role is negotiation skills, design interview questions that assess candidates' experience and success in negotiating deals, overcoming objections, and closing sales.

4. Objective Decision-Making: Structured interviews promote objective decision-making by providing a clear evaluation framework. This reduces bias and subjective judgments, ensuring that hiring decisions are based on the candidates' qualifications and performance during the interview process. Example: Develop a scoring rubric or rating system that allows interviewers to objectively evaluate candidates' responses to each question or competency. Use this system to rank and compare candidates based on their demonstrated skills and qualifications.

5. Improved Hiring Outcomes: Implementing a structured interview process improves hiring outcomes by selecting candidates who are the best fit for the sales role and the organization. It increases the likelihood of hiring individuals who possess the necessary skills, experience, and traits required for success in driving sales and achieving targets. Example: Conduct panel interviews where multiple interviewers assess candidates collaboratively. This approach allows for a more comprehensive evaluation and reduces the risk of overlooking critical factors.

6. Positive Candidate Experience: A structured interview process enhances the candidate experience by providing a well-organized and professional assessment. It demonstrates your commitment to a thorough evaluation and can leave a positive impression on candidates, regardless of the final hiring decision. Example: Provide clear instructions to candidates before the interview, communicate the interview timeline, and promptly provide feedback and updates on their application status. This ensures a positive experience and enhances your employer brand.

Implementing a structured interview process is essential for assessing sales candidates effectively. By ensuring consistency, fairness, valid assessment, identifying key competencies, promoting objective decision-making, improving hiring outcomes, and providing a positive candidate experience, you can select top-performing sales professionals who align with your organization's needs. Develop a structured interview process that includes standardized questions, evaluation criteria, and scoring systems to make informed and unbiased hiring decisions that contribute to the success of your sales team.

Preparing Interview Questions and Scenarios

Preparing effective interview questions and scenarios is crucial for assessing sales candidates and gaining insights into their skills, experience, and suitability for the role. In this chapter, we will explore the process of crafting interview questions and scenarios that allow you to evaluate candidates' abilities, problem-solving skills, and sales techniques. We will provide examples and guidelines to help you create a comprehensive and insightful interview process.

Preparing Interview Questions and Scenarios:

1. Job-specific Questions: Craft interview questions that specifically relate to the sales role and the responsibilities associated with it. These questions should assess the candidate's understanding of the sales process, their approach to selling, and their ability to meet targets. Example: "Tell me about a time when you successfully turned a prospect into a long-term client. How did you build a relationship with the prospect, address their objections, and close the sale?"

2. Behavioral-based Questions: Use behavioral-based questions to evaluate a candidate's past performance and experiences. These questions require candidates to provide specific examples of how they have demonstrated relevant skills and competencies in their previous roles.

Example: "Describe a situation where you faced a difficult sales challenge. How did you handle it, and what steps did you take to overcome obstacles and achieve success?"

3. Role-play Scenarios: Incorporate role-play scenarios to assess a candidate's ability to handle sales interactions and demonstrate their sales techniques. Provide a realistic scenario that reflects a typical sales situation and observe how the candidate engages with the scenario, addresses objections, and closes the deal. Example: "You are a sales representative meeting with a potential client who has expressed concerns about the price of your product. Role-play the scenario and demonstrate how you would handle the objection and persuade the client to see the value of the product."

4. Problem-solving Questions: Include problem-solving questions to assess a candidate's ability to think critically, adapt to challenges, and find creative solutions. Present candidates with a hypothetical sales problem and ask them to outline their approach to resolving it. Example: "Imagine you are faced with a situation where a client is unhappy with the delivery time of their order and threatens to cancel the contract. How would you address the issue and retain the client's business?"

5. Situational Questions: Pose situational questions to assess how candidates would handle specific sales situations they may encounter in the role. These questions test the candidate's ability to analyze a scenario, make

informed decisions, and apply their sales skills effectively. Example: "You are meeting with a potential client who seems hesitant to commit. How would you build trust, address their concerns, and close the sale in this situation?"

6. Cultural Fit Questions: Include questions that assess a candidate's fit with the company culture and values. These questions evaluate how well candidates align with your organization's mission, work environment, and team dynamics. Example: "Our company values collaboration and teamwork. Can you share an example of how you have successfully worked as part of a team to achieve sales targets?"

Preparing interview questions and scenarios that assess sales candidates effectively is crucial for making informed hiring decisions. By including job-specific questions, behavioral-based questions, role-play scenarios, problem-solving questions, situational questions, and cultural fit questions, you can gain valuable insights into a candidate's skills, experience, problem-solving abilities, and alignment with your organization's values. Tailor your interview questions to the sales role and objectives, ensuring a comprehensive evaluation of candidates' sales capabilities. This will enable you to select top-performing sales professionals who are well-suited for your organization's sales team.

Step-by-Step Structured Interview Process

1. Pre-Interview Preparation:

✓ Identify the competencies and skills required for the sales role.

✓ Develop a list of interview questions that align with those competencies.
✓ Create a structured scoring rubric or evaluation criteria to assess candidates consistently.

Example: If one of the key competencies is "Customer Relationship Management," the interview question could be: *"Can you provide an example of a challenging customer relationship situation you successfully managed? How did you address the issue and maintain a positive customer relationship?"*

2. Introduction and Icebreaker:

✓ Welcome the candidate and briefly introduce yourself and the company.
✓ Create a comfortable and friendly environment by engaging in small talk or asking an icebreaker question.

Example: *"Thank you for coming today. Before we begin, how was your journey here? Did you have any trouble finding the location?"*

3. Background and Experience Assessment:

✓ Ask candidates to provide an overview of their relevant experience, educational background, and any specific sales achievements or accolades.
✓ Probe deeper into their experiences to gather more detailed information.

Example: *"Can you walk me through your sales experience, including the industries you've worked in and the types of products or services you've sold? What were some of your notable achievements or success stories?"*

4. Competency-Based Questions:

✓ Ask structured, competency-based questions that target the specific skills and competencies required for the sales role.
✓ Use the STAR method (Situation, Task, Action, Result) to guide candidates in providing detailed responses.

Example: *"Tell me about a time when you had to handle a difficult objection from a prospect. How did you respond, and what was the outcome? Walk me through the steps you took and the strategies you employed."*

5. Scenario-Based Questions:

✓ Present hypothetical scenarios or real-life sales situations and ask candidates how they would handle them.
✓ Evaluate their problem-solving abilities, sales strategies, and decision-making skills.

Example: *"Imagine you are pitching a product to a potential client who is hesitant due to budget constraints. How would you address their concerns and persuade them to invest in the product? Walk me through your approach."*

6. Cultural Fit and Teamwork Assessment:

✓ Ask questions to assess candidates' alignment with the company's values, culture, and ability to work collaboratively in a team environment.

Example: *"Our company values teamwork and collaboration. Can you share an experience where you actively contributed to a team's success and how you built strong working relationships with colleagues?"*

7. Candidate Questions:

✓ Provide an opportunity for candidates to ask questions about the company, the sales role, or any other relevant aspects.

✓ Evaluate their level of interest, engagement, and research preparation.

Example: *"Is there anything specific you would like to know about our company culture or the expectations for this sales role?"*

8. Conclusion:

✓ Thank the candidate for their time and participation.

✓ Inform them about the next steps in the hiring process and the timeline for decision-making.

Example: "*Thank you for taking the time to interview with us today. We will be reviewing all the candidates and will reach out to you within the next week to provide an update on the status of your application.*"

Note: Throughout the interview, take detailed notes and score candidates based on their responses and performance against the predetermined evaluation criteria. This structured approach ensures consistency and fairness in the assessment process, making it easier to compare candidates objectively and select the most suitable sales professionals for your team.

Interview Questions and Scenarios to ask a Sales Candidate during the Hiring Process

Here are 25 interview questions and scenarios to ask a sales candidate during the hiring process:

1. *Tell me about a time when you exceeded your sales target. What strategies did you use to achieve this?*

2. *Walk me through your process for generating leads and prospecting potential customers.*

3. *How do you handle objections from customers? Can you provide an example of a challenging objection you successfully overcame?*

4. *Describe a situation where you had to navigate a complex sales cycle with multiple decision-makers. How did you approach it?*

5. *How do you build and maintain relationships with clients? Can you share an example of a long-term client partnership you developed?*

6. *Give me an example of a challenging negotiation you conducted with a client. How did you reach a mutually beneficial agreement?*

7. *Tell me about a time when you had to sell a product or service that had a longer sales cycle. How did you stay motivated throughout the process?*

8. *How do you manage your time and prioritize tasks when dealing with multiple clients and sales opportunities?*

9. *Describe a situation where you had to handle a dissatisfied customer. How did you address their concerns and turn the situation around?*

10. *Walk me through your approach to conducting a needs analysis with a potential customer. How do you identify their pain points and match them with your product/service?*

11. *Share an example of a sales presentation you delivered that had a significant impact on a customer's decision to purchase.*

12. *How do you stay updated on industry trends and changes? Can you provide an example of*

how this knowledge helped you in a sales situation?

13. *Describe a time when you had to collaborate with other departments or teams to secure a sale. How did you coordinate efforts and ensure a successful outcome?*

14. *Give me an example of a difficult decision you had to make during the sales process. How did you weigh the options and come to a resolution?*

15. *How do you handle rejection and stay motivated in a challenging sales environment? Can you share an example?*

16. *Tell me about a time when you identified an up-selling or cross-selling opportunity with an existing customer. How did you approach it?*

17. *Walk me through your process for conducting a competitive analysis. How do you differentiate yourself from competitors in the sales process?*

18. *Give me an example of a time when you had to adapt your sales approach to a different market or customer segment.*

19. *Describe a situation where you had to handle a sales crisis or unexpected challenge. How did you mitigate the issue and maintain customer satisfaction?*

20. *How do you use data and analytics to measure and track your sales performance? Can you share an example of how data analysis influenced your sales strategy?*

21. *Tell me about a time when you had to meet tight deadlines or quotas. How did you manage your workload to achieve the desired results?*

22. *Share an example of a successful referral you obtained from an existing customer. How do you leverage referrals to expand your customer base?*
23. *Describe a time when you had to work with a difficult or demanding customer. How did you manage the situation and ensure a positive outcome?*
24. *How do you handle rejection and objections in cold-calling situations? Can you provide an example of a successful cold-calling experience?*
25. *Walk me through your approach to building and maintaining a sales pipeline. How do you ensure a steady flow of leads and opportunities?*

These questions and scenarios cover a range of sales-related skills, experiences, and challenges, allowing you to assess a candidate's suitability for the sales role and their ability to excel in various sales situations. Remember to adapt and customize these questions based on the specific requirements of your organization and the sales position you are hiring for.

Conducting Behavioral and Situational Interviews

Behavioral and situational interviews are powerful tools for assessing sales candidates' skills, experiences, and decision-making abilities. This chapter focuses on the importance of conducting these types of interviews and provides examples and guidelines to help you effectively evaluate sales candidates using behavioral and situational interview techniques.

Conducting Behavioral and Situational Interviews:

1. Behavioral Interviews: Behavioral interviews aim to assess how candidates have performed in specific situations in the past, providing insights into their behaviors, actions, and outcomes. These interviews focus on candidates' actual experiences rather than hypothetical scenarios. Example: "Tell me about a time when you had to meet an ambitious sales target. How did you approach the situation, and what actions did you take to achieve or exceed the goal? What was the outcome?"

2. Structuring Behavioral Interviews: To conduct effective behavioral interviews, follow these steps:

a) Identify the Competencies: Determine the key competencies required for the sales role and select specific behavioral questions that align with those competencies. Example: If one of the competencies is "relationship-building," ask candidates to share a situation where they successfully developed a long-term relationship with a client.

b) Use the STAR Method: Ask candidates to structure their responses using the STAR method (Situation, Task, Action, Result). This framework helps candidates provide a clear and organized explanation of their experiences. Example: "Can you describe a Situation or Task where you had to build a relationship with a difficult client? What Actions did you take, and what was the Result?"

c) Probing for Details: Encourage candidates to provide specific examples, quantify their achievements, and explain the impact of their actions. Ask follow-up questions to dig deeper into their experiences and gain a comprehensive understanding of their abilities. Example: "How did you measure the success of the relationship-building efforts? Can you provide specific figures on increased sales or client retention rates?"

3. Situational Interviews: Situational interviews assess candidates' problem-solving skills and ability to handle hypothetical scenarios they may encounter in the sales role. These interviews provide insight into candidates' critical thinking, decision-making, and sales strategies. Example: "You are assigned to a challenging sales territory with declining market share. How would you approach this situation to revitalize sales and regain market dominance?"

4. Structuring Situational Interviews: To conduct effective situational interviews, follow these steps:

a) Prepare Realistic Scenarios: Develop situational scenarios that mirror real-life challenges sales professionals commonly face. These scenarios should require candidates to analyze the situation, make informed decisions, and propose sales strategies. Example: "You are given a new product to sell in a highly competitive market. How would you position the product, differentiate it from competitors, and convince potential customers to choose your solution?"

b) Assess Decision-Making and Sales Approach: Ask candidates to explain their thought process, the factors they would consider, and the actions they would take to address the scenario. Evaluate their ability to apply sales techniques, adapt to challenges, and achieve desired outcomes. Example: "How would you prioritize your sales activities in a situation where you have multiple leads and limited time? How would you ensure maximum productivity and effectiveness?"

c) Encourage Justification and Strategy Explanation: Ask candidates to justify their decisions and explain the strategies they propose. Evaluate their ability to articulate their reasoning and provide a clear sales-focused approach. Example: "Can you explain why you would choose that particular sales approach in the given scenario? What are the expected benefits and potential challenges?"

Conducting behavioral and situational interviews is essential for assessing sales candidates effectively. By structuring these interviews, using the STAR method for behavioral questions, preparing realistic situational scenarios, and probing for details, you can gain valuable insights into candidates' past experiences, decision-making skills, and sales strategies. This approach enables you to identify top-performing sales professionals who possess the necessary competencies and can thrive in challenging sales environments. Conduct behavioral and situational interviews with a fair and consistent approach, ensuring that you gather the information needed to make informed hiring decisions for your sales team.

Examples of Behavioral and Situational Interviews Questions to Assess Sales Candidates

Here are five examples each of behavioral and situational interview questions to assess sales candidates:

Behavioral Interview Questions:

1. *Describe a time when you faced a difficult sales situation. How did you handle it, and what was the outcome? What did you learn from that experience?*
2. *Tell me about a time when you had to build a relationship with a challenging client. How did you establish trust and overcome any obstacles to secure the sale?*
3. *Share an example of a time when you had to work collaboratively with colleagues or teams from other departments to achieve a sales goal. How did you ensure effective collaboration and achieve a successful outcome?*
4. *Describe a situation where you had to adapt your sales approach to meet the needs of a specific customer or market segment. How did you customize your sales strategy, and what results did you achieve?*
5. *Tell me about a time when you faced a setback or rejection in a sales situation. How did you handle it emotionally, and what steps did you take to bounce back and continue pursuing your sales goals?*

Situational Interview Questions:

1. *Imagine you are meeting a potential client for the first time. How would you approach the*

initial conversation to build rapport and establish a foundation for future sales discussions?

2. *You have a limited budget to attend a trade show and generate leads. How would you prioritize your activities and ensure maximum return on investment in terms of lead generation and sales opportunities?*

3. *Suppose a customer raises concerns about your product's price compared to competitors. How would you address the objection and communicate the value proposition to convince the customer to choose your product?*

4. *You have a sales presentation scheduled with a high-level executive who has limited time and is skeptical about your product's benefits. How would you structure your presentation to capture their attention and address their skepticism effectively?*

5. *Imagine you are assigned to sell a new product or service that hasn't gained much market awareness. How would you develop a sales strategy to create interest and generate demand among potential customers?*

These behavioral and situational interview questions help assess a candidate's past experiences, skills, and problem-solving abilities in real-life scenarios. Their responses will provide insights into their approach to sales challenges, adaptability, customer-centricity, collaboration skills, and resilience. Remember to ask follow-up questions to dig deeper into their thought process and evaluate their sales acumen and suitability for the role.

Evaluating Sales Skills and Competencies

Evaluating sales skills and competencies is crucial in the assessment process of sales candidates. This chapter focuses on the importance of evaluating key sales skills and competencies and provides examples and guidelines to help you effectively assess candidates' abilities in these areas.

Evaluating Sales Skills and Competencies:

1. Active Listening: Effective sales professionals must possess strong listening skills to understand customer needs, address concerns, and tailor their sales approach accordingly. Assess candidates' ability to actively listen and demonstrate understanding during the interview. Example: "Can you share an instance where you actively listened to a customer's needs and used that information to provide a personalized sales solution?"

2. Communication Skills: Strong communication skills are essential for sales professionals to articulate product features, benefits, and value propositions. Evaluate candidates' ability to communicate clearly, persuasively, and adapt their communication style to different audiences. Example: "Please describe a situation where you effectively communicated complex information to a customer who initially had difficulty understanding the product's benefits."

3. Relationship Building: Assess candidates' relationship-building abilities as sales professionals need to establish trust, rapport, and long-term partnerships with clients. Evaluate their skills in cultivating and nurturing relationships. Example: "Tell me about a time

when you successfully built strong relationships with customers. How did you establish trust, and what strategies did you employ to maintain those relationships over time?"

4. Problem-Solving: Sales professionals encounter various challenges and objections during the sales process. Evaluate candidates' problem-solving skills by presenting them with hypothetical scenarios or past sales situations they may have faced. Example: "How would you handle a customer who has multiple objections to purchasing your product? Walk me through your problem-solving approach in addressing those objections."

5. Resilience and Persistence: Sales can be a demanding and competitive field. Assess candidates' resilience and persistence in overcoming obstacles, handling rejection, and staying motivated in a sales environment. Example: "Describe a time when you faced significant sales setbacks. How did you stay motivated and bounce back from those challenges?"

6. Negotiation Skills: Evaluate candidates' negotiation skills, as successful sales professionals must be able to navigate negotiations, address objections, and close deals effectively. Example: "Can you share an example of a successful negotiation you conducted with a customer? How did you reach a mutually beneficial agreement?"

7. Sales Process Knowledge: Assess candidates' understanding of the sales process and their ability to follow a structured

approach in qualifying leads, conducting needs assessments, and closing sales. Example: "Explain the steps you typically follow in the sales process from initial prospecting to closing a deal. How do you ensure a smooth progression?"

8. Goal Orientation: Sales professionals should be driven by goals and targets. Evaluate candidates' goal orientation, their track record in achieving sales targets, and their strategies for exceeding expectations. Example: "Describe a time when you set ambitious sales goals for yourself. How did you stay motivated and ultimately achieve or surpass those targets?"

Evaluating sales skills and competencies is critical in assessing the suitability of candidates for sales roles. By assessing key competencies such as active listening, communication skills, relationship building, problem-solving, resilience, negotiation skills, sales process knowledge, and goal orientation, you can gain a comprehensive understanding of candidates' abilities and potential for success in driving sales. Tailor your evaluation methods, such as asking targeted questions and reviewing candidates' past achievements, to assess these competencies effectively. This will enable you to select top-performing sales professionals who possess the necessary skills and competencies to excel in your sales team.

Examples of Evaluating Sales Skills and Competencies when Assessing Sales Candidates

Here are five examples of evaluating sales skills and competencies when assessing sales candidates:

1. Role-Play Exercise: Conduct a role-play exercise where the candidate plays the role of a salesperson and you play the role of a potential customer. Assess their ability to engage in effective communication, ask probing questions, handle objections, and close the sale.

2. Presentation Assessment: Ask candidates to prepare and deliver a sales presentation on a given topic. Evaluate their presentation skills, ability to articulate key messages, demonstrate product knowledge, and engage the audience.

3. Sales Metrics Analysis: Provide candidates with sales data or scenarios and ask them to analyze the metrics. Evaluate their ability to interpret sales data, identify trends, and make data-driven decisions to improve sales performance.

4. Negotiation Simulation: Simulate a negotiation scenario where the candidate needs to negotiate a deal with a potential customer. Assess their negotiation skills, ability to find win-win solutions, and maintain a positive relationship while maximizing value for the company.

5. Sales Strategy Discussion: Engage candidates in a discussion about their approach to developing a sales strategy. Assess their understanding of target market segmentation, value proposition development, competitive analysis, and their ability to align sales strategies with organizational goals.

These evaluation methods provide opportunities to assess specific sales skills and competencies such as communication, negotiation, presentation, data analysis, strategic thinking, and relationship building. By observing candidates in action and analyzing their responses, you can gain valuable insights into their abilities and potential for success in the sales role. Remember to provide clear evaluation criteria and score candidates based on their performance against those criteria.

Administering Sales Assessments and Tests

Introduction: Administering sales assessments and tests is an effective way to evaluate the skills, knowledge, and aptitude of sales candidates. This chapter focuses on the importance of using assessments and tests in the assessment process and provides examples and guidelines to help you effectively evaluate sales candidates through these methods.

Administering Sales Assessments and Tests:

1. Personality Assessments: Personality assessments help you understand candidates' traits, motivations, and work preferences, providing insights into their fit within your sales team and their sales approach. Example: Use a personality assessment tool to evaluate candidates' extraversion, assertiveness, resilience, and problem-solving tendencies.

2. Sales Aptitude Tests: Sales aptitude tests assess candidates' natural sales abilities, such as their verbal and numerical reasoning, problem-solving skills, and ability to handle sales scenarios. Example: Administer a sales

aptitude test that includes questions related to sales calculations, logical reasoning, and situational judgment.

3. Role-Play Exercises: Role-play exercises simulate real-life sales scenarios and allow candidates to showcase their sales skills, negotiation abilities, and objection handling techniques. Example: Assign candidates a role-play scenario where they have to engage with a potential client and navigate through objections to close a deal.

4. Sales Knowledge Assessments: Sales knowledge assessments evaluate candidates' understanding of sales principles, techniques, and product/service knowledge. Example: Administer a sales knowledge assessment that includes questions about the sales process, customer relationship management, objection handling, and product/service features.

5. Presentation or Pitching Exercises: Presentation or pitching exercises assess candidates' ability to deliver persuasive sales presentations, effectively communicate product benefits, and engage with potential clients. Example: Ask candidates to prepare and deliver a sales presentation on a given product or service, evaluating their ability to engage the audience, present key points, and address questions.

6. Role-Specific Assessments: Tailor assessments to specific sales roles, such as inside sales, field sales, or account management, to evaluate candidates' suitability for the particular position. Example:

For an inside sales role, administer an assessment that includes phone-based sales scenarios and cold-calling exercises.

7. CRM Simulations: CRM simulations assess candidates' proficiency in using customer relationship management software, which is crucial for managing customer interactions and tracking sales activities. Example: Provide candidates with a simulated CRM system and ask them to perform tasks such as entering customer data, tracking leads, and generating sales reports.

8. Behavioral Assessments: Behavioral assessments measure candidates' behaviors, values, and motivations, providing insights into their cultural fit and potential for success in the sales role. Example: Utilize a behavioral assessment tool to evaluate candidates' teamwork, adaptability, resilience, and customer-centric behaviors.

Administering sales assessments and tests is a valuable component of the candidate assessment process. By utilizing personality assessments, sales aptitude tests, role-play exercises, sales knowledge assessments, presentation or pitching exercises, role-specific assessments, CRM simulations, and behavioral assessments, you can gain a comprehensive understanding of candidates' sales capabilities, aptitude, knowledge, and fit within your sales team. Tailor these assessments to the specific requirements of the sales role to ensure accurate evaluation. Remember to use these assessments in conjunction with other assessment methods, such as interviews and reference checks, to make informed decisions when hiring top-performing sales professionals.

Sales Assessments and Tests when Assessing Sales Candidates

When assessing sales candidates, there are various types of assessments and tests that can be administered to evaluate their sales abilities and aptitude. Here are some examples:

1. Sales Aptitude Test: This test assesses a candidate's natural aptitude for sales by evaluating their cognitive abilities, problem-solving skills, and numerical reasoning. It helps gauge their potential for success in a sales role. Example: A numerical reasoning question could be: "You have a product with a price of $50 and a cost of $30. What is the profit margin percentage?"

Specific example for **'Sales Aptitude Test'**

A sales aptitude test assesses a candidate's natural aptitude for sales by evaluating their cognitive abilities, problem-solving skills, and numerical reasoning. Here are some examples of questions you might find in a sales aptitude test:

- ✓ Numerical Reasoning: Example Question: You have a product with a price of $50 and a cost of $30. What is the profit margin percentage? Options: a) 20% b) 30% c) 40% d) 50%

This question assesses a candidate's ability to perform basic calculations and analyze numerical data, which is crucial for understanding profit margins and financial aspects of sales.

- ✓ Logical Reasoning: Example Question: Complete the following analogy: Salesperson is to persuasive as __________ is to creative.

Options: a) Artist b) Scientist c) Analyst d) Writer

This question evaluates a candidate's ability to identify logical relationships and make accurate associations, which is important for developing persuasive and creative sales strategies.

✓ Problem-Solving: Example Question: You have a prospect who has expressed interest in your product but is concerned about the price. How would you address their concern and demonstrate the value of your product? Options: a) Offer a discount to match their budget b) Explain the long-term benefits and cost savings of your product c) Provide testimonials from satisfied customers who have achieved significant results with your product d) Offer a free trial period to showcase the value and ROI of your product

This question tests a candidate's ability to think critically and come up with effective solutions to address customer concerns, which is essential for successful sales negotiations and objection handling.

✓ Sales Scenario Analysis: Example Question: You have a list of 100 leads. How would you prioritize and segment them to maximize your sales efforts and increase conversion rates? Options: a) Randomly contact leads until you reach the desired sales target b) Prioritize leads based on their industry and market size c) Prioritize leads based on their engagement level with your marketing materials d) Prioritize leads based on their geographic location and proximity to your sales team

This question assesses a candidate's ability to analyze and strategize the most efficient and effective approach to lead prioritization and segmentation, which is crucial for optimizing sales efforts and achieving targets.

These examples illustrate the types of questions you may encounter in a sales aptitude test. The test helps identify candidates who possess the cognitive abilities and problem-solving skills necessary for success in a sales role. Remember to select questions that align with the specific skills and competencies required for your sales position and industry.

2. Personality Assessment: A personality assessment measures a candidate's behavioral traits and tendencies, providing insights into their communication style, interpersonal skills, resilience, and adaptability. It helps determine how well they may fit into a sales role and engage with customers. Example: The assessment may include questions that ask candidates to rate their agreement or disagreement with statements such as "I enjoy meeting new people and building relationships" or "I am comfortable taking risks and handling rejection."

3. Sales Skills Assessment: This assessment evaluates a candidate's specific sales skills, such as prospecting, objection handling, closing techniques, and relationship-building abilities. It typically involves scenario-based questions or role-playing exercises. Example: Candidates may be asked to handle objections from a potential customer during a simulated sales call or to demonstrate their closing techniques in a role-play scenario.

4. Situational Judgment Test (SJT): An SJT presents candidates with realistic work-related scenarios and asks them to choose the most appropriate course of action. It assesses their judgment, problem-solving skills, and ability to handle sales-specific situations. Example: Candidates may be presented with a scenario where a customer is dissatisfied with a product and asked to select the best response from a set of options, considering factors such as customer service, product knowledge, and relationship management.

5. Product Knowledge Assessment: This assessment tests a candidate's knowledge about the product or service they will be selling. It evaluates their understanding of key features, benefits, competitive advantages, and how they can effectively communicate these to potential customers. Example: Candidates may be asked multiple-choice questions about product specifications, industry trends, or customer use cases to assess their level of product knowledge.

These assessments provide objective data points to supplement interviews and help evaluate candidates' sales-related skills, aptitude, personality traits, and product knowledge. It's important to select assessments that align with the specific requirements of the sales role and your organization's sales process.

Chapter 6
Conducting
Effective Sales Interviews

Conducting Effective Sales Interviews

Building Rapport and Creating a Positive Atmosphere

The interview is a crucial stage in the hiring process, as it allows you to assess a candidate's qualifications, skills, and cultural fit for your sales team. In this chapter, we will explore strategies for building rapport and creating a positive atmosphere during sales interviews. By establishing a comfortable environment, you can encourage candidates to showcase their true abilities and provide valuable insights for making informed hiring decisions.

1. Creating a Welcoming Environment:
- ✓ Start the interview with a warm greeting and introductions.
- ✓ Offer candidates a comfortable seating arrangement and ensure a well-lit and noise-free environment.
- ✓ Use positive body language and maintain eye contact to convey interest and engagement.

Example: *"Welcome to the interview! I'm delighted to have you here. Please have a seat, and let's get started."*

2. Establishing Rapport:
- ✓ Begin the interview with small talk to put candidates at ease and build a connection.
- ✓ Show genuine interest in their background, experiences, and achievements.
- ✓ Listen actively and respond empathetically to establish a rapport.

Example: "Before we dive into the interview questions, I'd love to learn more about your previous sales experience. Can you share some highlights or achievements that you're proud of?"

3. Asking Open-Ended Questions:
- ✓ Utilize open-ended questions to encourage candidates to provide detailed responses and insights.
- ✓ Allow candidates to share their thought processes, approaches, and strategies.
- ✓ Probe deeper into their experiences and seek specific examples to validate their claims.

Example: *"Tell me about a challenging sales situation you faced and how you overcame it. What strategies did you use, and what was the outcome?"*

4. Active Listening and Clarification:
- ✓ Practice active listening to demonstrate genuine interest in candidates' responses.
- ✓ Paraphrase their answers and seek clarification to ensure a thorough understanding.
- ✓ Ask follow-up questions to explore specific aspects of their experiences or achievements.

Example: *"If I understand correctly, you mentioned that you successfully closed a major deal by implementing a customized solution. Could you elaborate on the specific steps you took to customize the solution to the customer's needs?"*

5. Providing Feedback and Encouragement:
- ✓ Offer positive reinforcement and feedback during the interview to create a supportive environment.
- ✓ Acknowledge candidates' achievements, skills, or unique perspectives.

✓ Provide opportunities for candidates to address any concerns or questions they may have.

Example: *"I appreciate the innovative approach you shared for prospecting new clients. Your creative thinking demonstrates the kind of problem-solving skills we value in our sales team."*

6. Closing the Interview:

✓ Summarize the key points discussed during the interview.

✓ Allow candidates to ask any final questions they may have.

✓ Express appreciation for their time and interest in the position.

Example: *"Before we conclude, let's recap some of the highlights from our conversation. I appreciate your thoughtful responses and insights. Do you have any final questions for me?"*

By implementing these strategies, you can create a positive and engaging atmosphere during sales interviews. This approach encourages candidates to feel comfortable, showcase their skills, and provide valuable insights, enabling you to make well-informed hiring decisions. Remember, building rapport is a two-way process, so be authentic and genuinely interested in candidates' experiences and perspectives.

Interview Question Templates- Samples

Here are some interview question templates that you can use as a starting point for different stages of the interview process:

General Interview Questions:

- ✓ *Can you tell me about yourself and your experience in sales?*
- ✓ *What motivates you to pursue a career in sales?*
- ✓ *How do you handle rejection or difficult situations in a sales environment?*
- ✓ *Can you share an example of a successful sales achievement you're proud of?*
- ✓ *How do you stay updated on industry trends and changes?*

Behavioral Interview Questions:

- ✓ *Describe a time when you faced a challenging sales situation. How did you handle it?*
- ✓ *Give an example of a time when you successfully built and maintained strong relationships with clients.*
- ✓ *Tell me about a time when you exceeded sales targets and how you achieved those results.*
- ✓ *Can you recall a situation where you had to handle a difficult customer? How did you resolve it?*
- ✓ *Share a situation where you had to collaborate with a team to achieve a sales goal. How did you contribute to the team's success?*

Situational Interview Questions:

- ✓ *Imagine you're facing a highly competitive market. How would you differentiate yourself and win customers over?*
- ✓ *Suppose you have a potential client who is hesitant to make a purchase. How would you convince them of the value and close the sale?*
- ✓ *If you encounter resistance from a prospect during a sales call, how would you handle*

objections and persuade them to move forward?

✓ *In a scenario where a customer is dissatisfied with your product or service, how would you address their concerns and retain their business?*

✓ *Suppose you're assigned a new territory with low customer engagement. What strategies would you implement to increase sales and market penetration?*

Technical/Role-specific Interview Questions:

✓ *What sales methodologies or techniques do you use to approach new prospects?*

✓ *How do you qualify leads and determine which opportunities to prioritize?*

✓ *Can you explain your process for developing a sales pipeline and managing it effectively?*

✓ *What tools or software do you use to track and analyze sales data?*

✓ *In your experience, what are the key factors that contribute to successful sales negotiations?*

Remember, these question templates are just starting points, and you can tailor them to fit the specific requirements of your sales role and company. Additionally, it's important to ask follow-up questions to dig deeper into a candidate's responses and assess their suitability for the position.

Active Listening and Effective Communication

Active listening and effective communication are essential skills for conducting successful sales interviews. In this chapter, we will explore techniques and strategies to enhance your active listening abilities and communicate effectively with sales candidates. By mastering these skills, you can gather meaningful information, understand candidates' capabilities, and make informed hiring decisions.

1. Demonstrate Attentive Body Language:

- ✓ Maintain eye contact to convey interest and engagement.
- ✓ Nod occasionally to show understanding and encouragement.
- ✓ Avoid distractions and focus solely on the candidate.

Example: *"I'm fully present and interested in what you have to say. Please go ahead."*

2. Use Verbal and Nonverbal Cues:

- ✓ Encourage candidates to continue by using verbal cues like "Go on" or "Tell me more."
- ✓ Provide nonverbal cues such as leaning forward or nodding to show you are actively listening.
- ✓ Use brief verbal affirmations like "I see" or "I understand" to acknowledge their responses.

Example: *"That's interesting. Can you provide more details about how you handled objections in that situation?"*

3. Practice Reflective Listening:

- ✓ Reflect candidates' responses by paraphrasing or summarizing their points.
- ✓ Show that you have understood their perspective and are actively processing the information.
- ✓ Seek confirmation or clarification to ensure accuracy.

Example: *"If I understand correctly, you faced a challenging sales situation and used a consultative approach to understand the customer's needs. Is that correct?"*

4. Ask Probing Questions:

- ✓ Ask open-ended questions to encourage candidates to elaborate on their experiences and thought processes.
- ✓ Use follow-up questions to dig deeper into specific details or seek examples to validate their claims.
- ✓ Avoid interrupting and allow candidates to fully express their thoughts.

Example: *"Can you provide an example of a time when you successfully negotiated a complex deal? What strategies did you use, and what was the outcome?"*

5. Practice Empathy and Emotional Intelligence:

- ✓ Demonstrate empathy by acknowledging and understanding candidates' emotions.
- ✓ Show genuine interest in their experiences and challenges.
- ✓ Adapt your communication style to match the candidate's personality and emotional cues.

Example: *"I can imagine that managing objections from potential customers can be challenging. How do you typically handle objections and maintain a positive rapport with clients?"*

6. Maintain a Two-Way Dialogue:

- ✓ Strike a balance between actively listening and engaging in the conversation.
- ✓ Ask relevant follow-up questions based on candidates' responses.
- ✓ Provide opportunities for candidates to ask their own questions and address any concerns.

Example: *"Before we move on, is there anything specific you would like to know about our sales team or the company culture?"*

By applying these active listening and effective communication techniques, you can foster a productive and meaningful dialogue with sales candidates during interviews. These skills allow you to gather valuable information, understand candidates' capabilities, and assess their fit for the sales role. Remember, effective communication is a two-way street, so ensure you actively participate in the conversation while giving candidates the space to express themselves fully.

Assessing Sales Candidates' Motivation and Drive

Assessing the motivation and drive of sales candidates is crucial to determining their potential success in a sales role. In this chapter, we will explore techniques and strategies for effectively evaluating candidates' motivation and drive during sales interviews. By understanding their level of motivation, you can identify individuals who are self-driven, resilient, and eager to achieve sales targets.

1. Ask Motivational Questions:
- ✓ Inquire about what motivates candidates to excel in a sales role.
- ✓ Explore their personal goals and how they align with the sales profession.
- ✓ Assess their drive to overcome challenges and achieve targets.

Example: *"What motivates you to pursue a career in sales? Can you share a specific experience that highlights your determination and drive to succeed?"*

2. Assess Goal Orientation:

✓ Determine candidates' goal-setting practices and their ability to set and achieve targets.
✓ Evaluate their level of ambition and their track record in meeting or exceeding goals.
✓ Understand their approach to handling setbacks and staying focused on objectives.

Example: *"Tell me about a time when you set a challenging sales goal for yourself. How did you go about achieving it, and what were the results?"*

3. Explore Resilience and Persistence:

✓ Evaluate candidates' resilience in the face of rejection and obstacles.
✓ Assess their ability to maintain a positive attitude and stay motivated during difficult times.
✓ Look for examples of how they persisted in reaching their goals despite setbacks.

Example: *"Sales can be a demanding and challenging field. Can you share a situation where you faced rejection or encountered a setback? How did you handle it, and what did you learn from the experience?"*

4. Evaluate Self-Drive and Proactivity:

✓ Determine candidates' level of self-motivation and their ability to take initiative.
✓ Assess their willingness to go the extra mile to achieve sales targets.
✓ Look for evidence of their proactive approach to identifying and pursuing new sales opportunities.

Example: *"How do you stay motivated and self-driven in your sales role? Can you provide an example of a time when you took initiative to close a deal or explore new markets without being prompted to do so?"*

5. Gauge Passion for Sales:

- ✓ Assess candidates' enthusiasm and passion for the sales profession.
- ✓ Explore their knowledge of sales techniques, strategies, and industry trends.
- ✓ Determine if they have a genuine interest in understanding customer needs and providing value through sales.

Example: *"What do you find most exciting and rewarding about a career in sales? How do you stay updated on sales best practices and industry trends?"*

By employing these techniques, you can effectively assess the motivation and drive of sales candidates during interviews. Understanding their level of motivation, goal orientation, resilience, self-drive, and passion for sales will help you identify individuals who are likely to thrive in a sales role and consistently strive to achieve sales targets. Remember to delve deeper into candidates' past experiences and ask for specific examples to validate their claims.

Questions to Assess a Sales Candidates' Motivation and Drive

1. *What initially attracted you to a career in sales? Can you tell me more about your motivation to pursue this profession?*
2. *How do you set and prioritize your sales goals? Can you provide an example of a challenging sales goal you set for yourself and how you achieved it?*
3. *How do you handle rejection and setbacks in sales? Can you share an experience where*

you faced a significant obstacle and how you overcame it?

4. *Tell me about a time when you went above and beyond to meet a sales target or exceed expectations. What motivated you to put in that extra effort?*
5. *How do you stay motivated and driven in your sales role, especially during times when the sales cycle is long or prospects are difficult to convert?*
6. *Can you provide an example of a situation where you proactively identified and pursued a new sales opportunity? What motivated you to take that initiative?*
7. *What strategies do you use to maintain a positive attitude and resilience in the face of rejection or challenging sales situations?*
8. *How do you stay updated on sales techniques, industry trends, and best practices? Can you share specific actions you take to continuously develop your sales skills?*
9. *What role does self-discipline play in your approach to achieving sales targets? How do you ensure you stay focused and productive in your daily sales activities?*
10. *Can you describe a situation where you demonstrated exceptional drive and determination to close a difficult sale? What steps did you take, and what was the outcome?*

When assessing a sales candidate's motivation and drive, these questions can help you gauge their level of enthusiasm, goal orientation, resilience, self-drive, and passion for sales. Pay attention to the specific examples and stories they share, as they can provide insights into their mindset and work ethic. Look for candidates who demonstrate a proactive and persistent attitude towards achieving sales targets and who possess a genuine passion for the sales profession.

Evaluating Sales Experience and Track Record

Evaluating the sales experience and track record of candidates is crucial to assessing their capabilities and potential for success in a sales role. In this chapter, we will explore techniques and strategies for effectively evaluating candidates' sales experience during interviews. By examining their past performance, achievements, and sales metrics, you can gain valuable insights into their ability to meet targets and drive revenue.

1. Review their Sales Experience:
- ✓ Begin by asking candidates to provide an overview of their sales experience, including the industries they have worked in and the types of products or services they have sold.
- ✓ Explore the length of their tenure with previous employers to assess their stability and commitment to sales roles.
- ✓ Inquire about their experience in both new business development and account management to determine their versatility.

Example: *"Can you walk me through your sales experience, highlighting the industries you've worked in and the types of products or services you've sold? How long have you typically stayed with each employer, and what roles have you held in terms of new business development and account management?"*

2. Seek Specific Achievements and Results:

- ✓ Ask candidates to provide specific examples of their most notable sales achievements, such as exceeding sales targets, closing significant deals, or winning awards.
- ✓ Inquire about the size and complexity of the deals they have handled to understand the scope of their responsibilities.
- ✓ Request quantitative metrics, such as revenue generated, sales growth percentages, or market share expansion, to assess their impact on business outcomes.

Example: *"Tell me about a sales achievement you're particularly proud of. Can you provide specific details about the deal size, the challenges you faced, and the results you achieved? How did your success contribute to the overall business goals?"*

3. Evaluate Sales Techniques and Strategies:

- ✓ Probe candidates on their sales techniques and strategies, including their approach to prospecting, relationship building, and closing deals.
- ✓ Assess their understanding of the sales process, including their ability to identify and qualify leads, handle objections, and negotiate effectively.
- ✓ Look for evidence of consultative selling, solution-oriented approaches, and the ability to adapt to different customer needs and preferences.

Example: *"Can you describe your typical sales approach? How do you go about prospecting and identifying potential clients? How do you handle objections and navigate the sales process to successfully close deals?"*

4. Assess Customer Relationship Management:
- ✓ Inquire about candidates' experience in building and maintaining long-term customer relationships.
- ✓ Evaluate their ability to understand customer needs, provide tailored solutions, and ensure customer satisfaction.
- ✓ Ask for examples of how they have managed customer accounts, upsold or cross-sold products/services, and secured repeat business.

Example: *"Tell me about a time when you successfully built and nurtured a long-term customer relationship. How did you understand their needs and provide value throughout the sales cycle? What strategies did you use to secure repeat business?"*

5. Analyze Sales Territory Management:
- ✓ Assess candidates' ability to effectively manage sales territories or assigned accounts.
- ✓ Inquire about their strategies for prioritizing leads, managing pipelines, and maximizing sales opportunities within their territories.
- ✓ Look for evidence of strategic planning, goal setting, and the ability to identify growth opportunities in untapped markets.

Example: *"How have you managed your sales territory or account base in previous roles? How did you prioritize leads and opportunities? Can you provide an example of how you maximized sales within your assigned territory?"*

By employing these techniques, you can effectively evaluate the sales experience and track record of candidates during interviews. Pay attention to specific achievements, results, sales techniques, customer relationship management, and sales territory management. Look for candidates who have a proven track record of meeting or exceeding sales targets, possess a strong understanding of the sales process, and demonstrate the ability to build successful customer relationships.

Questions to Evaluate a Sales candidate's Experience and Track Record

1. *Can you provide an overview of your sales experience, including the industries you've worked in and the types of products or services you've sold?*
2. *What were your specific sales targets in your previous roles, and how consistently did you meet or exceed them?*
3. *Can you share a specific example of a challenging sale or deal you successfully closed? What was the deal size, and how did it contribute to your overall sales performance?*
4. *How do you approach prospecting and generating new leads? Can you provide an example of a successful lead generation strategy you implemented?*
5. *Tell me about a time when you faced a difficult objection from a prospect. How did you handle it, and what was the outcome?*
6. *Describe your process for managing and nurturing customer relationships. How do you ensure customer satisfaction and retention?*
7. *Can you share a situation where you successfully upsold or cross-sold additional products or services to an existing customer?*

What strategies did you use to identify those opportunities?

8. *How do you manage your sales pipeline and prioritize your leads? Can you explain your approach to managing multiple prospects simultaneously?*
9. *Have you been involved in territory or account management? How did you strategically plan and allocate your time and resources to maximize sales within your assigned territory?*
10. *Tell me about a time when you faced a significant sales challenge or setback. How did you overcome it, and what did you learn from the experience?*

These questions will help you assess a sales candidate's experience and track record. By asking about their previous sales roles, achievements, target attainment, lead generation strategies, objection handling, customer relationship management, up-selling/cross-selling, pipeline management, and how they handle challenges, you can gain valuable insights into their capabilities, adaptability, and past successes in driving sales results.

Addressing Potential Red Flags and Concerns

Introduction: During the sales interview process, it is essential to address any potential red flags or concerns that may arise regarding a candidate's suitability for the sales role. In this chapter, we will discuss strategies and examples for effectively addressing these issues, allowing you to make informed decisions when hiring sales professionals.

1. Exploring Gaps in Employment History:

- ✓ If a candidate has gaps in their employment history, inquire about the reasons behind those gaps.
- ✓ Look for explanations that demonstrate personal growth, professional development, or relevant experiences during those periods.
- ✓ Evaluate whether the candidate's skills and qualifications remained current during the gaps.

Example: *"I noticed a six-month gap in your employment history. Can you please explain what you were doing during that time? Were there any activities or experiences that contributed to your professional development or helped you enhance your sales skills?"*

2. Handling Job Hopping:

- ✓ If a candidate has a history of frequent job changes, ask for their reasons behind each transition.
- ✓ Look for valid justifications, such as seeking career advancement, personal growth, or better opportunities.
- ✓ Assess their level of commitment and stability by evaluating the duration of their previous roles.

Example: *"I see that you have had a few job changes within the past couple of years. Can you provide some insight into the reasons behind those transitions and what you were hoping to achieve with each move?"*

3. Addressing Performance Issues:

- ✓ If a candidate's past performance metrics or references raise concerns, address them directly.

- ✓ Inquire about specific situations and seek explanations for any underperformance.
- ✓ Look for candidates who take responsibility, demonstrate a willingness to learn from their mistakes, and have shown growth in subsequent roles.

Example: *"One of your references mentioned that there were some performance challenges in a previous role. Can you provide some context around those issues and how you addressed them? What did you learn from that experience, and how have you improved since then?"*

4. Handling Over-qualification:

- ✓ If a candidate appears overqualified for the role, discuss their motivations and expectations.
- ✓ Determine if they are genuinely interested in the position and assess their willingness to commit to the responsibilities.
- ✓ Look for candidates who can clearly articulate why they believe this role aligns with their career goals.

Example: *"Given your extensive experience and qualifications, why are you interested in this particular sales role? How do you see this opportunity contributing to your professional growth and development?"*

5. Assessing Cultural Fit:

- ✓ Inquire about the candidate's understanding of your company's culture and values.
- ✓ Look for alignment between their values and the organization's culture.
- ✓ Evaluate their ability to adapt to different work environments and collaborate effectively with colleagues.

Example: *"Our company places a strong emphasis on teamwork and collaboration. Can you share a situation where you worked successfully in a team-based sales environment? How do you see yourself fitting into our company culture?"*

By addressing potential red flags and concerns during the sales interview process, you can gain a better

Questions to Uncover any Potential Red Flags and Concerns of Sales Candidates

1. *Can you explain any gaps in your employment history? What were you doing during those periods?*
2. *I noticed that you've had several job changes in the past few years. Can you provide some insights into the reasons behind those transitions?*
3. *In one of your previous roles, there were references to performance issues. Can you provide some context around those challenges and how you addressed them?*
4. *How do you handle rejection or setbacks in sales? Can you give an example of a difficult situation you faced and how you overcame it?*
5. *Can you explain why you're interested in this particular sales role? What about it appeals to you?*
6. *What are your expectations for career growth and development in this position? How does it align with your long-term goals?*
7. *How do you handle stress and pressure in a sales environment? Can you give an example*

of a high-pressure situation you encountered and how you managed it?

8. *Can you share an experience where you had to work with a challenging client or customer? How did you handle the situation, and what was the outcome?*

9. *How do you manage your time and prioritize tasks in a fast-paced sales role? Can you provide an example of how you've successfully managed multiple deadlines or projects simultaneously?*

10. *Our company values teamwork and collaboration. Can you share an experience where you worked successfully in a team-based sales environment? How do you contribute to a positive team dynamic?*

These questions can help uncover potential red flags or concerns during the sales interview process. By addressing gaps in employment history, job hopping, performance issues, motivation for the role, stress management, and teamwork, you can gain a deeper understanding of the candidate's suitability for the position and assess their ability to overcome challenges.

Chapter 7
Making the Right Offer

Making the Right Offer

Determining Competitive Compensation Packages

We will now discuss the importance of determining competitive compensation packages when making job offers to sales professionals. We will explore various factors to consider, strategies for determining compensation, and examples to guide you in making the right offer.

1. Understanding the Importance of Competitive Compensation:

- ✓ Competitive compensation is crucial for attracting top sales talent and ensuring their motivation and satisfaction.
- ✓ Sales professionals are often driven by financial incentives, making compensation a significant factor in their decision to join or stay with a company.
- ✓ A well-structured compensation package can incentivize salespeople to achieve their targets and contribute to the company's success.

Example: *"Competitive compensation is vital in attracting and retaining high-performing sales professionals. It not only serves as a motivating factor but also rewards their efforts and drives their commitment to achieving sales goals."*

2. Factors to Consider in Determining Compensation:

- ✓ Benchmark industry standards and salary ranges to gain an understanding of market rates for similar sales roles.

- ✓ Consider the level of experience, skills, and qualifications required for the position.
- ✓ Assess the complexity and competitiveness of the sales territory or market the candidate will be working in.
- ✓ Account for additional incentives such as commissions, bonuses, and performance-based rewards.

Example: *"When determining compensation, it is essential to consider industry standards, the candidate's experience, and the specific demands of the sales role. We should also evaluate the potential for performance-based incentives to align with our company's goals and motivate sales professionals."*

3. Designing a Competitive Compensation Package:

- ✓ Offer a base salary that is competitive and aligns with the candidate's experience and market rates.
- ✓ Structure commission or bonus plans that provide an attractive earning potential based on achieving sales targets.
- ✓ Consider offering additional perks or benefits such as health insurance, retirement plans, or car allowances.
- ✓ Provide clear guidelines on performance expectations and how the compensation package can be maximized.

Example: *"Our competitive compensation package includes a base salary that is commensurate with your experience and the market rates for this role. Additionally, we offer a commission structure that rewards high-performance and a comprehensive benefits package to support your well-being and financial goals."*

4. Negotiating Compensation:

- ✓ Be open to discussing compensation expectations with the candidate.
- ✓ Clearly communicate the components of the compensation package, including base salary, commission structure, and benefits.
- ✓ Discuss any flexibility within the compensation range and evaluate the candidate's qualifications and negotiation skills.

Example: *"We understand that compensation is an important consideration for you. Let's have a conversation about your salary expectations and how we can structure a compensation package that meets your needs and aligns with our company's guidelines."*

5. Compliance with Legal and Ethical Standards:

- ✓ Ensure that your compensation practices comply with local labor laws and regulations.
- ✓ Avoid discriminatory practices and ensure fairness and equality in compensation.
- ✓ Maintain transparency and integrity throughout the negotiation process.

Example: *"As an organization, we are committed to maintaining compliance with all applicable laws and regulations regarding compensation. We adhere to ethical standards and promote fairness and equality in our compensation practices."*

By understanding the importance of competitive compensation, considering various factors, designing an attractive package, and maintaining compliance with legal and ethical standards, you can make the right offer to sales professionals. Remember to align compensation with performance incentives, balance market rates with the candidate's qualifications, and communicate the value of the overall package effectively.

Negotiating Sales Salaries and Commission Structures

Introduction: In Chapter 7, we will delve into the crucial process of negotiating sales salaries and commission structures when making job offers to sales professionals. We will explore strategies for successful negotiations, considerations for salary and commission structures, and examples to guide you in making the right offer.

1. Understanding the Importance of Negotiation:

- ✓ Negotiation is a key aspect of the hiring process, especially when it comes to sales salaries and commission structures.
- ✓ Both parties, the employer and the candidate, aim to reach an agreement that satisfies their needs and aligns with market standards.
- ✓ Successful negotiation ensures that the compensation package is competitive, motivating, and fair for both parties.

Example: *"Negotiation plays a pivotal role in the hiring process as it allows us to find a mutually beneficial agreement that reflects the candidate's qualifications and market standards. A successful negotiation sets the foundation for a positive working relationship and incentivizes the sales professional to excel."*

2. Strategies for Negotiating Sales Salaries:

- ✓ Research industry salary benchmarks and understand the candidate's market value based on their experience, skills, and qualifications.

✓ Determine the maximum salary you are willing to offer while considering budget constraints and the position's value to the company.
✓ Clearly communicate the base salary range to the candidate and be prepared to justify the offered amount based on market data and the candidate's fit for the role.
✓ Highlight additional benefits or perks that can enhance the overall compensation package.

Example: *"Based on our research and market standards, we have determined a competitive salary range for this position. We believe the proposed salary reflects your qualifications and the value you would bring to our organization. Additionally, we offer comprehensive benefits that provide further value and support your professional growth."*

3. Considerations for Commission Structures:

✓ Assess the company's sales goals and objectives to determine the appropriate commission structure.
✓ Design a commission plan that aligns with the sales role's responsibilities and encourages performance and goal achievement.
✓ Clearly define the commission structure, including commission rates, thresholds, and any accelerators or bonuses for exceeding targets.
✓ Communicate the potential earning opportunities and the correlation between performance and commission earnings.

Example: *"Our commission structure is designed to reward high-performance and align with our sales objectives. It includes a competitive commission rate based on achieved sales targets, with additional incentives for surpassing expectations. This structure offers significant earning potential for motivated and successful sales professionals."*

4. Effective Negotiation Techniques:

- ✓ Actively listen to the candidate's expectations and concerns regarding salary and commission.
- ✓ Remain flexible and open to compromise, while also considering the company's financial constraints.
- ✓ Explore alternative forms of compensation, such as performance bonuses, equity, or career development opportunities.
- ✓ Focus on the candidate's overall package and the value the position and company offer beyond just financial compensation.

Example: *"We understand that compensation is an important consideration for you, and we are committed to finding a mutually beneficial agreement. While we have budget limitations, we are open to discussing alternative forms of compensation that may be of value to you, such as additional performance bonuses or opportunities for professional growth."*

5. Closing the Negotiation:

- ✓ Reach a final agreement that satisfies both parties' needs and expectations.
- ✓ Document the agreed-upon salary, commission structure, and any additional benefits or terms discussed.
- ✓ Communicate the finalized offer clearly and promptly to the candidate to ensure a smooth transition into the organization.

Example: *"After carefully considering your qualifications and our budget, we are pleased to extend an offer with a base salary of $X and a* *commission structure that aligns with our sales goals. Additionally, you will receive comprehensive benefits that include X, X, and X. We believe this offer represents a fair and competitive compensation package for your expertise and contributions."*

By understanding the importance of negotiation, employing effective strategies, considering salary and commission structures, and employing successful negotiation techniques, you can make the right offer to sales professionals. Remember to balance market standards with the candidate's qualifications, remain open to compromise, and ensure clear communication throughout the negotiation process.

Presenting a Compelling Job Offer

Introduction: In Chapter 7, we will explore the crucial process of presenting a compelling job offer to sales professionals. We will discuss the key elements of a job offer, strategies for effective presentation, and examples to guide you in making a compelling offer that attracts top sales talent.

1. Understanding the Elements of a Compelling Job Offer:

- ✓ Salary and Commission: Clearly outline the base salary, commission structure, and potential for earnings based on performance.
- ✓ Benefits and Perks: Highlight the comprehensive benefits package, including health insurance, retirement plans, paid time off, and any additional perks.
- ✓ Career Development Opportunities: Emphasize the opportunities for growth,

training, and advancement within the organization.

- ✓ Company Culture and Values: Showcase the company's culture, values, and mission to create a sense of alignment and purpose for the candidate.

Example: *"Our compelling job offer encompasses a competitive base salary and commission structure that rewards high performance. You will also have access to a comprehensive benefits package, including health insurance, retirement plans, and ample opportunities for professional development. As part of our company culture, we emphasize collaboration, innovation, and making a positive impact in the industry."*

2. Strategies for Effective Presentation:

- ✓ Personalize the offer: Tailor the job offer to the candidate's specific needs and preferences based on their motivations and priorities.
- ✓ Highlight unique selling points: Emphasize what sets your organization apart from competitors and why it is an attractive opportunity for the candidate.
- ✓ Create a positive atmosphere: Present the offer in a warm and engaging manner, ensuring the candidate feels valued and excited about the opportunity.
- ✓ Provide supporting documentation: Include all relevant documents such as the offer letter, benefits package details, and any additional information the candidate may need.

Example: *"We have customized this job offer to align with your goals and aspirations. Our organization stands out for its innovative product offerings, strong market presence, and commitment to employee development. We are thrilled to present you with this offer, and we believe it offers a compelling package that reflects your expertise and potential."*

3. Addressing Candidate Questions and Concerns:

- ✓ Be prepared to address any questions or concerns the candidate may have regarding the job offer.
- ✓ Provide clarity on any ambiguous aspects, such as commission calculation, performance expectations, or career progression.
- ✓ Showcase the company's commitment to supporting employee success and satisfaction.

Example: *"We understand that you may have questions or concerns about the job offer. We are here to provide you with all the necessary information and address any queries you may have. Our organization is dedicated to transparency and fostering a supportive environment to ensure your success and satisfaction."*

4. Prompt and Professional Communication:

- ✓ Communicate the job offer promptly to avoid leaving the candidate in a state of uncertainty.
- ✓ Ensure the offer is delivered in a professional manner, either in person or through a formal email or offer letter.
- ✓ Provide a reasonable timeframe for the candidate to consider the offer and make a decision.

Example: *"Congratulations! We are delighted to extend this job offer to you. Please find attached the offer letter, which outlines the details of the position, compensation, benefits, and next steps. We kindly request your response within [specified timeframe] to ensure a smooth on-boarding process."*

5. Flexibility and Negotiation:
- ✓ Be open to negotiating certain aspects of the job offer, such as salary, benefits, or start date, to accommodate the candidate's needs and demonstrate flexibility.
- ✓ Clearly communicate any limitations or boundaries to avoid unrealistic expectations.

Example: *"While we have put together a competitive offer, we are open to discussing certain aspects to ensure a mutually beneficial agreement. If there are specific areas you would like to discuss further, please let us know, and we will do our best to accommodate your needs within our parameters."*

By incorporating these strategies and presenting a compelling job offer that addresses the candidate's needs, highlights unique selling points, and fosters a positive atmosphere, you can increase the likelihood of attracting top sales talent and securing their acceptance.

Handling Counteroffers and Resolving Conflicts

We will now explore the critical process of handling counteroffers and resolving conflicts that may arise during the job offer stage. We will discuss strategies for effectively managing counteroffers, addressing candidate concerns, and finding resolutions that satisfy both parties. By understanding how to navigate these challenges, you can increase the chances of securing top sales talent.

1. Understanding Counteroffers:
- ✓ A counteroffer is when a candidate receives a job offer from your company but decides to

negotiate with their current employer for better terms.
- ✓ Counteroffers can create challenges and uncertainty in the hiring process, as they can entice candidates with improved compensation or other benefits.
- ✓ It is essential to be prepared to handle counteroffers effectively to ensure a successful outcome.

Example: *"Counteroffers are a common occurrence in the hiring process. We understand that candidates may receive enticing offers from their current employers, and it is important for us to address any concerns or conflicts that arise to secure the best talent for our organization."*

2. Responding to Counteroffers:
- ✓ Maintain open communication with the candidate to understand their motivations for considering a counteroffer.
- ✓ Reinforce the reasons why your offer aligns with the candidate's career goals and the unique opportunities your organization provides.
- ✓ Address any concerns the candidate may have regarding the offer and clarify any points of ambiguity.
- ✓ Reiterate the value and growth potential that your organization offers beyond just financial compensation.

Example: *"We appreciate that you are considering a counteroffer. We believe our offer is a reflection of your qualifications and the exciting opportunities we provide. Our organization offers a supportive environment, career growth prospects, and the chance to make a significant impact in the industry.*

We are committed to ensuring your long-term success and job satisfaction."

3. Resolving Conflicts:

- ✓ Foster open and honest dialogue with the candidate to understand their concerns and address them proactively.
- ✓ Seek mutually beneficial resolutions by exploring alternatives that meet both parties' needs, such as adjusting compensation, providing additional benefits, or offering flexible work arrangements.
- ✓ Maintain a solution-oriented mindset and focus on finding common ground to reach a resolution that satisfies both the candidate and the company.

Example: *"We understand that conflicts may arise during the offer stage. Our priority is to find a resolution that satisfies both parties. Let's discuss your concerns and explore potential solutions together. We are open to considering adjustments to the offer, such as adjusting the compensation package or providing additional benefits to ensure a mutually beneficial outcome."*

4. Importance of Flexibility:

- ✓ Demonstrate flexibility and willingness to accommodate reasonable requests from the candidate.
- ✓ Communicate any limitations or boundaries to manage expectations effectively.
- ✓ Be open to considering alternative solutions that may address the candidate's concerns while maintaining the company's best interests.

Example: *"We understand the importance of flexibility during this stage of the hiring process.*

While we strive to meet your needs, we also have certain limitations to consider. We are open to discussing potential adjustments or alternatives that would address your concerns while aligning with the company's policies and objectives."

5. Timely Decision-Making:

- ✓ Encourage the candidate to make an informed decision within a reasonable timeframe.
- ✓ Provide any additional information or support the candidate may require to facilitate their decision-making process.
- ✓ Maintain regular communication to keep the candidate engaged and informed throughout the decision-making period.

Example: *"We understand that making a decision involves careful consideration. We kindly request that you inform us of your decision within [specified timeframe]. If there is any additional information you need to help you make your decision, please let us know, and we will be happy to provide it promptly."*

By following these strategies and effectively managing counteroffers and conflicts, you can navigate through potential challenges and ensure a smooth and successful job offer process. Remember to maintain open communication, explore mutually beneficial resolutions, and prioritize the candidate's needs while safeguarding the interests of the company.

Chapter 8
On-boarding and Training New Sales Hires

On-boarding and Training New Sales Hires

Developing an Effective On-boarding Process

In this chapter, we will explore the crucial process of on-boarding and training new sales hires. We will discuss the importance of a well-designed on-boarding program, key elements to include, and strategies for effectively integrating new sales professionals into your organization. By developing an effective on-boarding process, you can set your new hires up for success and accelerate their productivity.

1. Understanding the Importance of On-boarding:
- ✓ On-boarding is the process of integrating new hires into your organization, familiarizing them with their role, the company culture, and providing the necessary resources and training for success.
- ✓ A well-designed on-boarding program ensures that new sales hires feel supported, valued, and equipped to perform their job effectively.
- ✓ Effective on-boarding contributes to higher employee engagement, faster ramp-up time, and increased retention rates.

Example: On-boarding is a critical component of the hiring process. It plays a vital role in setting the stage for new sales hires to thrive in their roles, embrace the company culture, and contribute to organizational success. By investing in a comprehensive on-boarding program, we can ensure a smooth transition for our new sales professionals and position them for long-term success.

2. Key Elements of an Effective On-boarding Process:

- ✓ Preparing for the arrival of the new hire: Set up their workspace, ensure necessary equipment and tools are ready, and provide any pre-boarding materials or instructions.
- ✓ Welcome and orientation: Introduce the new hire to their team members, provide an overview of the company's mission, values, and culture, and familiarize them with company policies and procedures.
- ✓ Role-specific training: Provide comprehensive training that covers product knowledge, sales methodologies, CRM systems, and any other tools or processes relevant to their role.
- ✓ Mentorship and buddy programs: Assign a mentor or buddy to the new hire to provide guidance, support, and assistance during the on-boarding period.
- ✓ Ongoing feedback and support: Regularly check in with the new hire to provide feedback, address questions or concerns, and ensure they have the necessary resources and support to excel in their role.

Example: Our on-boarding process comprises several key elements to ensure a seamless integration for our new sales hires. We begin by preparing their workspace and providing pre-boarding materials to familiarize them with our organization. During their first week, we conduct a comprehensive orientation program, including introductions to the team and an overview of our company culture. We then provide role-specific training to equip them with the necessary skills and knowledge to excel in their sales role. Throughout the on-boarding period, they will have a dedicated mentor who will guide and support them, and we will provide ongoing feedback and support to facilitate their growth and success.

3. Strategies for Effective On-boarding:

- ✓ Establish clear objectives and expectations: Clearly communicate the goals and expectations for the on-boarding period, ensuring the new hire understands what they need to accomplish and how their progress will be measured.
- ✓ Provide a structured timeline: Develop a detailed on-boarding schedule that outlines the activities, training sessions, and milestones the new hire will experience during their on-boarding period.
- ✓ Encourage engagement and interaction: Foster a sense of belonging by providing opportunities for the new hire to interact with their colleagues, attend team meetings, and participate in collaborative projects.
- ✓ Continuous learning and development: Offer ongoing learning and development opportunities to help the new hire further enhance their skills and knowledge beyond the initial on-boarding period.
- ✓ Seek feedback: Regularly solicit feedback from the new hire about their on-boarding experience, identifying areas for improvement and making necessary adjustments.

Example: To ensure the effectiveness of our on-boarding process, we have implemented various strategies. We establish clear objectives and expectations from the start, providing the new hire with a roadmap for success. We provide a structured timeline that outlines their on-boarding activities and training sessions, ensuring they have a clear understanding of what to expect. We encourage engagement and interaction by facilitating opportunities for them to collaborate with their colleagues. Additionally, we emphasize continuous learning and development, offering ongoing training and support beyond the initial on-boarding period. Lastly, we value their feedback and regularly seek input to refine and improve our on-boarding process.

By implementing these strategies and developing an effective on-boarding process, you can ensure that your new sales hires integrate smoothly into the organization, feel supported, and become productive contributors to your sales team.

Providing Sales Training and Product Knowledge

We will focus on the crucial aspect of providing sales training and product knowledge to new sales hires during the on-boarding process. We will explore the importance of comprehensive sales training, strategies for delivering effective training programs, and the significance of product knowledge in driving sales success. By prioritizing sales training and equipping new hires with in-depth product knowledge, you can set them up for success and empower them to achieve their sales targets.

1. The Importance of Comprehensive Sales Training:

- ✓ Sales training is essential for new hires to develop the skills, techniques, and strategies necessary to excel in their sales role.
- ✓ Comprehensive sales training ensures that new sales hires are equipped with the knowledge and tools they need to effectively engage with prospects, overcome objections, and close deals.
- ✓ A well-designed sales training program enhances the new hire's confidence, competence, and overall sales performance.

Example: Comprehensive sales training is a critical component of our on-boarding process. We recognize that providing our new sales hires with the necessary skills and knowledge is essential for their success in driving sales revenue. By investing in comprehensive sales training, we can equip our sales team with the tools and techniques needed to excel in their roles and achieve outstanding results.

2. Strategies for Delivering Effective Sales Training:

- ✓ Customize the training program: Tailor the sales training program to align with the specific needs of your organization, industry, and sales process.
- ✓ Blend various training methods: Incorporate a mix of interactive sessions, role-playing exercises, case studies, and e-learning modules to engage new hires and reinforce learning.
- ✓ Utilize experienced trainers: Leverage the expertise of experienced sales professionals or trainers who can effectively convey sales best practices, share real-world examples, and provide valuable insights.

- ✓ Provide ongoing coaching and support: Offer continuous coaching and support to reinforce learning, address individual challenges, and provide guidance throughout the on-boarding period.
- ✓ Incorporate feedback and assessment: Gather feedback from new hires regarding the effectiveness of the training program and make necessary adjustments. Conduct assessments to measure their understanding and application of the training concepts.

Example: Our sales training program is designed to deliver effective learning experiences for our new sales hires. We customize the program to align with our unique sales process, industry, and target market. We blend various training methods to create an interactive and engaging environment. Experienced trainers, who have a deep understanding of our sales strategies, deliver the training, incorporating real-world examples and case studies. We provide ongoing coaching and support to ensure continuous learning and improvement. Additionally, we gather feedback from our new hires to assess the effectiveness of the training program and make necessary enhancements.

3. The Significance of Product Knowledge:

- ✓ Product knowledge is a fundamental component of a sales professional's success. It enables them to effectively communicate the value proposition, address customer pain points, and position the product as a solution.
- ✓ Comprehensive product knowledge instills confidence in the sales team, allowing them to engage in meaningful conversations with prospects and provide accurate information.

✓ Regular updates and refreshers on product knowledge are essential to keep the sales team up to date with the latest features, enhancements, and competitive advantages of the product.

Example: Product knowledge is a cornerstone of our sales training. We believe that a deep understanding of our products and their value proposition is crucial for our sales team's success. We provide extensive training on our products, including features, benefits, and competitive advantages. We ensure our sales team has access to the most up-to-date product information through regular updates and refreshers. By equipping our sales team with in-depth product knowledge, we empower them to confidently engage with prospects and effectively communicate the value our products offer.

By prioritizing comprehensive sales training and providing in-depth product knowledge, you can ensure that your new sales hires have the skills, confidence, and expertise to drive sales success. This investment in their development will contribute to their overall effectiveness in achieving sales targets and building strong customer relationships.

Setting Clear Expectations and Performance Goals

We will explore how establishing clear expectations and goals can drive motivation, accountability, and performance. By effectively communicating expectations and setting achievable goals, you can empower your new sales hires to strive for excellence and contribute to the success of your organization.

1. Establishing Clear Expectations:

- ✓ Clearly communicate the responsibilities, roles, and expectations for new sales hires.
- ✓ Provide a detailed overview of the job requirements, sales targets, and key performance indicators.
- ✓ Outline the expected behaviors, work ethic, and professional conduct.

Example: At our company, we believe in setting clear expectations from the start. We provide new sales hires with a comprehensive overview of their roles and responsibilities, emphasizing the importance of their contribution to our sales success. We communicate our expectations regarding sales targets, key performance indicators, and the desired behaviors and work ethic. By establishing clear expectations, we create a foundation for success and align our new sales hires with our organization's goals.

2. Setting Performance Goals:

- ✓ Collaborate with new sales hires to set realistic and achievable performance goals.
- ✓ Align individual goals with the overall sales team objectives.
- ✓ Ensure that goals are specific, measurable, attainable, relevant, and time-bound (SMART goals).

Example: During the on-boarding and training process, we work closely with our new sales hires to set performance goals. We encourage them to contribute their input and actively participate in the goal-setting process. We ensure that the goals are aligned with the overall sales team objectives and are specific, measurable, attainable, relevant, and time-bound. By setting performance goals, we provide a roadmap for success and motivate our sales hires to strive for excellence.

3. Monitoring and Providing Feedback:

- ✓ Regularly monitor the progress of new sales hires towards their goals.
- ✓ Provide constructive feedback and guidance to help them improve their performance.
- ✓ Recognize and celebrate milestones and achievements along the way.

Example: We believe in continuous monitoring and feedback as part of our on-boarding and training process. We closely track the progress of our new sales hires towards their performance goals. We provide timely and constructive feedback to guide them in refining their skills and improving their performance. We also make it a point to recognize and celebrate their milestones and achievements, fostering a positive and motivating environment.

4. Adjusting Goals as Needed:

- ✓ Assess the progress and performance of new sales hires regularly.
- ✓ Adjust goals and expectations based on individual development, market conditions, and organizational changes.
- ✓ Provide support and resources to help them overcome challenges and meet revised goals.

Example: We understand that circumstances and priorities may change over time. Therefore, we regularly evaluate the progress and performance of our new sales hires. If necessary, we make adjustments to their goals and expectations based on individual development, market conditions, and organizational changes. We provide the necessary support, resources, and training to help them overcome challenges and meet the revised goals.

By setting clear expectations and performance goals for your new sales hires, you provide them with a roadmap for success and create a culture of accountability and achievement. This, in turn, fosters their development, motivates their performance, and contributes to the overall success of your sales team and organization.

Establishing Mentorship and Coaching Programs

This part focuses on the significance of establishing mentorship and coaching programs for new sales hires during the on-boarding and training process. We will explore how mentorship and coaching can enhance the learning experience, accelerate skill development, and drive sales success. By providing guidance, support, and opportunities for growth through mentorship and coaching, you can empower your new sales hires to excel in their roles and contribute to the success of your organization.

1. The Importance of Mentorship:

- ✓ Mentorship provides new sales hires with a trusted advisor who can offer guidance, support, and insights based on their experience.
- ✓ Mentors can help new hires navigate challenges, understand the organizational culture, and accelerate their learning curve.
- ✓ Mentorship fosters a sense of belonging, engagement, and personal growth for new sales hires.

Example: At our organization, we recognize the value of mentorship in the on-boarding and training process. We pair each new sales hire with a seasoned sales professional who serves as their mentor. This mentor provides guidance, support, and a wealth of industry knowledge. By establishing mentorship, we create a supportive environment where new sales hires can learn, grow, and thrive.

2. Implementing a Coaching Program:

- ✓ Coaching programs provide ongoing support and development opportunities for new sales hires.
- ✓ Coaches can help new hires refine their sales skills, overcome obstacles, and achieve their goals.
- ✓ Regular coaching sessions allow for continuous feedback, skill enhancement, and performance improvement.

Example: In addition to mentorship, we implement a comprehensive coaching program for our new sales hires. Each new hire is assigned a coach who works closely with them to refine their sales skills, provide feedback, and offer guidance. These coaching sessions focus on skill development, goal setting, and addressing any challenges that may arise. By incorporating coaching, we ensure that our new sales hires receive the support and resources they need to excel in their roles.

3. Structured Mentorship and Coaching Activities:

- ✓ Develop a structured mentorship and coaching program with defined goals and activities.
- ✓ Establish regular meetings, both one-on-one and group sessions, to facilitate mentorship and coaching interactions.

- ✓ Provide resources, tools, and training materials to support mentorship and coaching activities.

Example: Our mentorship and coaching program is designed with structured activities and goals in mind. We facilitate regular one-on-one meetings between mentors and new sales hires to foster a strong mentorship relationship. Additionally, we organize group sessions where new hires can interact with their peers and mentors to share experiences, best practices, and lessons learned. We also provide resources such as training materials, playbooks, and online tools to support the mentorship and coaching activities.

4. Measuring the Effectiveness of Mentorship and Coaching:

- ✓ Establish metrics and evaluation methods to measure the impact of mentorship and coaching programs.
- ✓ Solicit feedback from new hires and mentors/coaches to assess the program's effectiveness.
- ✓ Make adjustments and improvements based on feedback and evaluation results.

Example: We believe in continuously improving our mentorship and coaching programs. To measure their effectiveness, we establish metrics such as sales performance improvement, employee satisfaction, and retention rates. We regularly solicit feedback from new hires and mentors/coaches through surveys, interviews, and focus groups to assess the program's impact. Based on this feedback and evaluation results, we make necessary adjustments and improvements to enhance the mentorship and coaching experience.

By establishing mentorship and coaching programs, you provide new sales hires with valuable guidance, support, and growth opportunities. This investment in their development fosters their professional growth, accelerates their learning, and contributes to their long-term success within your organization.

Chapter 9
Retaining Top Sales Talent

Retaining Top Sales Talent

Recognizing the Importance of Employee Engagement

We will now explore the various aspects of employee engagement and how it directly impacts the motivation, productivity, and loyalty of your sales team. By recognizing the importance of employee engagement and implementing strategies to foster it, you can create a positive work environment that attracts and retains top sales talent.

1. Understanding Employee Engagement:
- ✓ Employee engagement refers to the emotional commitment and involvement of employees in their work and the organization.
- ✓ Engaged employees are passionate, motivated, and dedicated to their roles, resulting in increased productivity and performance.
- ✓ Employee engagement is influenced by factors such as job satisfaction, recognition, growth opportunities, and a positive work culture.

Example: At our organization, we place a strong emphasis on employee engagement. We understand that engaged employees are the foundation of a successful sales team. We foster an environment where employees feel motivated, supported, and recognized for their contributions. By prioritizing employee engagement, we create a workplace that attracts and retains top sales talent.

2. Recognizing the Benefits of Employee Engagement:

- ✓ Engaged employees are more likely to stay with the organization, reducing turnover and associated costs.
- ✓ Engaged employees are more productive, resulting in increased sales performance and revenue generation.
- ✓ Engaged employees create a positive work culture, influencing the morale and engagement of other team members.

Example: Studies have consistently shown the positive impact of employee engagement on organizational success. Engaged employees are more likely to stay with the organization, reducing turnover and the costs associated with hiring and training new sales professionals. They are highly motivated and productive, driving sales performance and contributing to revenue growth. Moreover, engaged employees create a positive work culture that inspires and motivates their colleagues.

3. Creating a Positive Work Environment:
- ✓ Foster a culture of trust, open communication, and collaboration.
- ✓ Provide opportunities for professional growth and development.
- ✓ Recognize and appreciate the achievements and contributions of your sales team.

Example: To promote employee engagement, we prioritize creating a positive work environment. We foster a culture of trust, where employees feel comfortable sharing ideas, concerns, and feedback. We encourage open communication and collaboration across the sales team. We provide ample opportunities for professional growth and development, such as training programs, mentorship, and skill-building workshops. Additionally, we recognize and appreciate the achievements and contributions of our sales team through regular rewards and recognition initiatives.

4. Regular Feedback and Performance Reviews:

- ✓ Conduct regular performance reviews to provide feedback and set goals.
- ✓ Offer constructive feedback and guidance for improvement.
- ✓ Recognize and celebrate successes and milestones.

Example: We understand the importance of regular feedback in fostering employee engagement. We conduct performance reviews to provide feedback on individual performance, set goals, and identify areas for improvement. We offer constructive feedback and guidance to help our sales team members excel in their roles. Additionally, we make it a point to recognize and celebrate their successes and milestones, further reinforcing their engagement and motivation.

5. Work-Life Balance and Well-being:

- ✓ Promote work-life balance initiatives, such as flexible working hours and remote work options.
- ✓ Support employee well-being through wellness programs and initiatives.
- ✓ Show genuine care and concern for the well-being of your sales team members.

Example: We recognize that work-life balance and employee well-being are crucial for maintaining high levels of engagement. We promote work-life balance by offering flexible working hours and remote work options, allowing our sales team members to manage their personal and professional responsibilities effectively. We also prioritize employee well-being by providing access to wellness programs and initiatives. Furthermore, we show genuine care and concern for the well-being of our sales team members, fostering a supportive and engaged work environment.

By recognizing the importance of employee engagement and implementing strategies to foster it, you can create a work environment that attracts and retains top sales talent. A highly engaged sales team leads to increased productivity, improved sales performance, and a positive work culture, contributing to the long-term success of your organization.

Creating a Positive Sales Culture

We will see how a strong sales culture influences employee satisfaction, motivation, and overall team performance. By cultivating a positive sales culture, you can create an environment where sales professionals thrive, stay engaged, and contribute to the success of your organization.

1. Defining a Positive Sales Culture:

- ✓ A positive sales culture encompasses shared values, beliefs, and behaviors that promote collaboration, growth, and success.
- ✓ It emphasizes teamwork, continuous learning, recognition, and a customer-centric approach.
- ✓ A positive sales culture creates an environment where sales professionals feel valued, motivated, and supported.

Example: At our organization, we understand the importance of a positive sales culture. We define it as a shared commitment to excellence, collaboration, and customer satisfaction. We foster an environment that encourages teamwork, innovation, and personal growth. By creating a positive sales culture, we aim to cultivate a work environment where our sales professionals can thrive and excel.

2. Leadership and Role Modeling:

- ✓ Leaders play a crucial role in shaping the sales culture by setting an example through their actions and behaviors.
- ✓ Leaders should embody the values and behaviors they expect from their sales team.
- ✓ They should provide clear direction, support, and recognition to foster a positive sales culture.

Example: Leadership plays a pivotal role in creating a positive sales culture. Our sales leaders lead by example, demonstrating the values and behaviors we expect from our sales professionals. They provide clear direction, support, and guidance to empower our sales team to succeed. Through their actions, they promote collaboration, growth, and a customer-centric approach, setting the tone for our positive sales culture.

3. Collaboration and Teamwork:

- ✓ Encourage collaboration and teamwork among sales professionals.
- ✓ Foster an environment where knowledge sharing, idea generation, and support are valued.
- ✓ Create opportunities for cross-functional collaboration to strengthen relationships and improve outcomes.

Example: In our sales culture, collaboration and teamwork are highly encouraged. We believe that working together leads to better results and a more supportive work environment. We foster a culture where sales professionals actively share knowledge, ideas, and best practices to help each other succeed. We also promote cross-functional collaboration, partnering with other departments to enhance customer experiences and drive overall organizational success.

4. Continuous Learning and Development:
- ✓ Provide opportunities for ongoing training, skill development, and professional growth.
- ✓ Offer resources such as workshops, webinars, and mentoring programs.
- ✓ Encourage a growth mindset that values continuous learning and improvement.

Example: In our positive sales culture, we prioritize continuous learning and development. We provide our sales team with opportunities for ongoing training and skill enhancement. This includes workshops, webinars, and access to industry experts. We also offer mentoring programs to support the professional growth of our sales professionals. By fostering a growth mindset and investing in their development, we ensure that our sales team stays at the forefront of industry trends and constantly improves their performance.

5. Recognition and Rewards:
- ✓ Recognize and reward sales professionals for their achievements and contributions.
- ✓ Celebrate individual and team successes to boost morale and motivation.
- ✓ Provide incentives and incentives aligned with performance goals to drive motivation and engagement.

Example: In our sales culture, we place a strong emphasis on recognition and rewards. We regularly acknowledge the achievements and contributions of our sales professionals. This can include individual performance milestones, exceeding targets, or demonstrating exceptional customer service. We celebrate these successes as a team, fostering a sense of pride and motivation. Additionally, we provide incentives and rewards aligned with performance goals, ensuring our sales team feels valued and motivated to achieve their best.

By creating a positive sales culture, you foster an environment where sales professionals thrive, stay engaged, and contribute to the success of your organization. A positive sales culture not only retains top sales talent but also enhances team collaboration, customer satisfaction, and overall business performance.

Offering Career Development and Growth Opportunities

We will get into how providing avenues for professional advancement and personal growth can increase employee satisfaction, loyalty, and motivation. By investing in the growth of your sales professionals, you create an environment that fosters continuous learning, career progression, and long-term commitment.

1. Assessing Individual Career Goals and Aspirations:
   ✓ Start by understanding the career goals and aspirations of your sales team members.
   ✓ Conduct regular discussions to assess their interests, strengths, and areas for development.
   ✓ Use this information to tailor career development plans that align with their goals.

Example: At our organization, we value the career aspirations of our sales professionals. We regularly engage in conversations to understand their individual goals, strengths, and areas for growth. This allows us to create personalized career development plans that cater to their specific ambitions and help them chart a path towards their desired career progression.

2.   Providing   Learning   and   Training Opportunities:
- ✓ Offer a variety of learning opportunities, such as workshops, seminars, online courses, and certifications.
- ✓ Create a training curriculum that addresses skill gaps and enhances sales capabilities.
- ✓ Encourage continuous learning by providing resources and platforms for self-directed learning.

Example: To support the growth of our sales professionals, we provide a range of learning and training opportunities. This includes workshops, seminars, online courses, and industry certifications. We have also developed a comprehensive training curriculum that focuses on enhancing sales skills and addressing specific areas for improvement. In addition, we provide access to online resources and platforms for self-directed learning, enabling our sales team to continuously expand their knowledge and capabilities.

3. Offering Stretch Assignments and Project Opportunities:
- ✓ Assign challenging projects or initiatives that allow sales professionals to develop new skills and broaden their experience.
- ✓ Provide opportunities to lead cross-functional teams, collaborate on strategic initiatives, or participate in special projects.

✓ These stretch assignments help individuals grow their skill set and demonstrate their potential for career advancement.

Example: We believe in offering stretch assignments and project opportunities to our sales professionals. By assigning them challenging projects outside their regular scope, we give them the chance to develop new skills and broaden their experience. This may involve leading cross-functional teams, collaborating on strategic initiatives, or participating in special projects. These opportunities not only foster personal growth but also showcase their capabilities for future career advancement.

4. Mentoring and Coaching Programs:
✓ Implement mentoring and coaching programs to provide guidance and support to sales professionals.
✓ Pair experienced mentors with less experienced individuals to facilitate knowledge transfer and career guidance.
✓ Offer regular coaching sessions to help sales professionals overcome challenges and develop their potential.

Example: As part of our commitment to career development, we have established mentoring and coaching programs for our sales professionals. Experienced mentors are paired with less experienced individuals to provide guidance, share insights, and offer career advice. We also conduct regular coaching sessions to help sales professionals address challenges, refine their skills, and unlock their full potential.

5. Internal Promotion and Advancement Opportunities:

- ✓ Create a culture that promotes internal promotions and advancement based on merit and performance.
- ✓ Provide clear pathways for career progression within the sales team, including roles with increased responsibilities and leadership opportunities.
- ✓ Communicate these advancement opportunities and encourage qualified individuals to pursue them.

Example: At our organization, we foster a culture that values internal promotions and advancement. We believe in recognizing and rewarding performance by providing clear pathways for career progression within our sales team. This includes roles with increased responsibilities, leadership opportunities, and the chance to lead strategic initiatives. We communicate these advancement opportunities to our sales professionals and actively encourage those who demonstrate the required skills and potential to pursue them.

By offering career development and growth opportunities, you create a supportive environment where sales professionals feel valued, motivated, and committed to their long-term success within the organization. This not only retains top sales talent but also strengthens the overall sales team and contributes to the growth of your business.

Providing Performance Feedback and Recognition

Effective feedback and recognition programs can enhance employee engagement, motivation, and job satisfaction. By implementing strategies that acknowledge and reward outstanding performance, you can create a culture of excellence and retain your top sales professionals.

1. Establishing a Feedback Culture:

- ✓ Foster a culture of open and regular feedback throughout the organization.
- ✓ Encourage managers and team members to provide constructive feedback on performance.
- ✓ Establish a feedback framework that emphasizes both positive reinforcement and areas for improvement.

Example: At our organization, we have established a feedback culture where open and regular communication is encouraged. We believe that providing feedback is crucial for the growth and development of our sales professionals. Our managers and team members are encouraged to give constructive feedback that highlights successes and identifies areas for improvement. We have implemented a feedback framework that balances positive reinforcement with opportunities for growth.

2. Conducting Regular Performance Reviews:

- ✓ Conduct formal performance reviews on a regular basis.
- ✓ Provide structured feedback on individual performance, strengths, and areas for development.
- ✓ Set goals and action plans for improvement based on the review discussions.

Example: We conduct regular performance reviews for our sales professionals. These reviews serve as a platform to provide structured feedback on individual performance. We discuss achievements, strengths, and areas for development. By setting clear goals and action plans during these reviews, we ensure that our sales professionals have a roadmap for continuous improvement and growth.

3. Recognizing Achievements and Milestones:

- ✓ Implement recognition programs to acknowledge and celebrate exceptional performance.
- ✓ Recognize individual sales achievements, milestones, and contributions to the team.
- ✓ Offer rewards, incentives, or public recognition to highlight outstanding performance.

Example: We have established a comprehensive recognition program to celebrate the achievements of our sales professionals. This program acknowledges individual sales accomplishments, significant milestones, and notable contributions to the team. We offer rewards, incentives, and public recognition to showcase and appreciate their outstanding performance. This recognition not only motivates our sales professionals but also reinforces a culture of excellence.

4. Providing Timely and Specific Feedback:

- ✓ Offer feedback in a timely manner to ensure its relevance and effectiveness.
- ✓ Be specific and provide actionable feedback that focuses on behaviors and outcomes.
- ✓ Communicate the impact of their performance on individual and team goals.

Example: We believe in providing timely and specific feedback to our sales professionals. By offering feedback promptly, we ensure its relevance and impact. We provide feedback that is specific, actionable, and focuses on behaviors and outcomes. We also communicate the direct impact of their performance on individual and team goals, helping them understand the significance of their contributions.

5. Encouraging Peer-to-Peer Recognition:
- ✓ Foster a culture of peer recognition where sales professionals appreciate and acknowledge each other's accomplishments.
- ✓ Encourage team members to give positive feedback and recognition to their peers.
- ✓ Implement platforms or programs that facilitate peer-to-peer recognition and appreciation.

Example: In addition to formal recognition programs, we encourage a culture of peer-to-peer recognition. We believe that recognizing the achievements of colleagues is equally important. Our sales professionals are encouraged to give positive feedback and recognition to their peers. We have implemented platforms and programs that facilitate peer-to-peer recognition, allowing our team members to appreciate and acknowledge each other's contributions.

By providing performance feedback and recognition, you create a supportive and motivating environment that fosters job satisfaction and retains top sales talent. Effective feedback and recognition programs demonstrate your commitment to the growth and success of your sales professionals, ultimately benefiting the overall performance of your sales team and organization.

Implementing Incentives and Rewards Programs

A well-designed incentive and reward program can motivate sales professionals, increase productivity, and enhance job satisfaction. By offering attractive incentives and rewards, you can create a culture of high performance and retain your top sales talent.

1. Understanding the Power of Incentives and Rewards:

- ✓ Recognize the impact of incentives and rewards in driving sales performance.
- ✓ Understand the different types of incentives, such as monetary bonuses, commissions, and non-monetary rewards.
- ✓ Realize the importance of aligning incentives with individual and organizational goals.

Example: Incentives and rewards play a crucial role in driving sales performance. They provide motivation, recognition, and a sense of accomplishment to sales professionals. We understand that incentives can take various forms, including monetary bonuses, commissions, and non-monetary rewards such as recognition or career advancement opportunities. By aligning these incentives with individual and organizational goals, we can create a rewarding environment that encourages top sales talent to thrive.

2. Designing a Comprehensive Incentive Program:

- ✓ Define clear and measurable performance metrics for sales professionals.
- ✓ Develop a tiered incentive structure that rewards different levels of achievement.
- ✓ Incorporate both individual and team-based incentives to foster collaboration.

Example: To implement an effective incentives and rewards program, it is essential to define clear and measurable performance metrics. These metrics can include sales revenue, customer acquisition, or other key performance indicators specific to your industry.

A tiered incentive structure can be designed to reward different levels of achievement, providing sales professionals with incremental incentives as they surpass targets. Additionally, incorporating team-based incentives encourages collaboration and a sense of shared success.

3. Tailoring Incentives to Individual Preferences:
- ✓ Understand that different sales professionals are motivated by different incentives.
- ✓ Offer a variety of incentives to cater to individual preferences.
- ✓ Provide flexibility in choosing rewards to accommodate diverse needs.

Example: We recognize that different sales professionals are motivated by different incentives. Some may be driven by financial rewards, while others value recognition or career development opportunities. To cater to these preferences, we offer a variety of incentives within our program. Sales professionals can choose between monetary bonuses, public recognition, additional vacation days, or professional development resources. This flexibility allows individuals to select rewards that align with their personal goals and aspirations.

4. Communicating Incentives and Rewards:
- ✓ Clearly communicate the details of the incentive program to all sales professionals.
- ✓ Highlight the benefits and potential rewards of achieving targets.
- ✓ Provide regular updates on performance and progress towards incentives.

Example: Effective communication is essential when implementing an incentives and rewards program. We ensure that all sales professionals are well-informed about the program, including its goals, criteria, and potential rewards. By highlighting the benefits of achieving targets, we create excitement and motivation within the sales team. Regular updates on performance and progress towards incentives keep everyone engaged and informed about their individual and team's performance.

5. Reviewing and Evaluating the Program:

- ✓ Continuously evaluate the effectiveness of the incentives and rewards program.
- ✓ Collect feedback from sales professionals to identify areas for improvement.
- ✓ Make necessary adjustments and enhancements to keep the program relevant and impactful.

Example: We believe in the importance of continuous improvement and evaluation of our incentives and rewards program. We collect feedback from sales professionals to gain insights into their experiences and suggestions for improvement. This feedback helps us identify areas where the program can be enhanced to better align with their needs and aspirations. Regular reviews and adjustments ensure that the program remains relevant and impactful in retaining top sales talent.

By implementing an effective incentives and rewards program, you create a competitive and engaging environment that fosters loyalty and motivation among your sales professionals. The right mix of incentives and rewards can drive performance, enhance job satisfaction, and ultimately retain top sales talent, benefiting the overall success of your sales team and organization.

Chapter 10
Managing and Evaluating Sales Performance

Managing and Evaluating Sales Performance

Setting Key Performance Indicators (KPIs)

We will now explore the importance of defining clear and measurable KPIs that align with organizational objectives. By effectively setting and tracking KPIs, sales managers can monitor and improve sales performance, drive productivity, and achieve desired outcomes.

1. Understanding the Role of Key Performance Indicators (KPIs):

- ✓ Define KPIs as measurable metrics that indicate sales performance and progress.
- ✓ Recognize the significance of KPIs in providing insights into sales effectiveness.
- ✓ Understand the correlation between KPIs and overall business success.

Example: Key Performance Indicators (KPIs) are quantifiable metrics that provide a snapshot of sales performance and progress. They serve as benchmarks to measure the effectiveness and efficiency of sales efforts. By setting and tracking relevant KPIs, sales managers gain insights into individual and team performance, enabling them to make data-driven decisions and drive business success.

2. Aligning KPIs with Organizational Objectives:

- ✓ Identify the specific objectives and goals of the sales team and organization.
- ✓ Map KPIs that directly align with these objectives.

✓ Ensure that KPIs are SMART (Specific, Measurable, Achievable, Relevant, Time-bound).

Example: To effectively manage sales performance, it is essential to align KPIs with the overall objectives of the sales team and organization. By clearly defining objectives such as revenue targets, market share growth, or customer acquisition, we can identify specific KPIs that directly reflect progress towards these goals. SMART KPIs ensure that they are Specific, Measurable, Achievable, Relevant, and Time-bound, providing a clear roadmap for sales performance evaluation.

3. Selecting Relevant KPIs:

✓ Identify KPIs that measure sales effectiveness, efficiency, and productivity.

✓ Consider a combination of leading and lagging indicators for a comprehensive view.

✓ Tailor KPIs to the unique needs and dynamics of the sales team and industry.

Example: To evaluate sales performance comprehensively, it is crucial to select relevant KPIs that reflect various aspects of sales effectiveness, efficiency, and productivity. Examples of leading indicators can include activities such as prospecting calls or sales presentations, while lagging indicators can encompass metrics like conversion rates or revenue growth. The selection of KPIs should be customized to the specific needs and dynamics of the sales team and industry.

4. Setting Clear Targets and Benchmarks:

✓ Establish specific targets and benchmarks for each KPI.

✓ Ensure that targets are challenging yet attainable.

- ✓ Regularly review and adjust targets based on performance and changing business conditions.

Example: To effectively manage and evaluate sales performance, it is vital to set clear targets and benchmarks for each KPI. These targets should be challenging enough to drive motivation and effort, but also attainable to ensure realistic expectations. Regularly reviewing and adjusting targets based on performance and changing business conditions allows for ongoing improvement and alignment with evolving objectives.

5. Monitoring and Tracking KPIs:

- ✓ Implement a system to track and monitor KPIs in real-time.
- ✓ Utilize technology and reporting tools to gather and analyze data.
- ✓ Regularly review and share KPI performance with the sales team.

Example: To manage and evaluate sales performance effectively, a robust system for monitoring and tracking KPIs is necessary. Utilizing technology and reporting tools, such as CRM software or dashboards, enables real-time data collection and analysis. Regular reviews of KPI performance provide opportunities to celebrate successes, identify areas for improvement, and make informed decisions to drive sales effectiveness.

By setting clear and relevant KPIs, aligning them with organizational objectives, and regularly monitoring and tracking performance, sales managers can effectively manage and evaluate sales performance, driving the success of their sales team and organization as a whole.

Setting Key Performance Indicators (KPIs) with Examples

Setting Key Performance Indicators (KPIs) for sales professionals is crucial for measuring and evaluating their performance. Here are some key considerations and examples of KPIs that can be used:

8. Revenue Generation:
- ✓ Monthly/Quarterly/Annual Sales Revenue: Measures the total revenue generated by the sales professional within a specific period.
- ✓ Average Deal Size: Tracks the average value of each sale closed by the sales professional.
- ✓ Sales Growth Rate: Evaluates the percentage increase in sales revenue over a defined period.

2. Sales Activities and Productivity:
- ✓ Number of Prospecting Calls: Measures the number of calls made by the sales professional to potential customers for lead generation.
- ✓ Number of Meetings/Demos: Tracks the number of meetings or product demonstrations conducted by the sales professional.
- ✓ Sales Conversion Rate: Calculates the percentage of leads or opportunities that result in a closed sale.

3. Customer Acquisition and Retention:
- ✓ Number of New Customers: Measures the number of new customers acquired by the sales professional.
- ✓ Customer Retention Rate: Tracks the percentage of existing customers retained by the sales professional.

✓ Customer Satisfaction Score: Assesses the satisfaction level of customers through surveys or feedback mechanisms.

4. Pipeline Management:
✓ Sales Pipeline Value: Measures the total value of potential deals in the sales professional's pipeline.
✓ Pipeline Conversion Rate: Evaluates the percentage of leads that progress through the sales pipeline and result in closed deals.
✓ Average Sales Cycle Length: Tracks the average duration it takes for a lead to move through the sales pipeline and convert into a sale.

5. Activity Efficiency:
✓ Time Spent Selling: Measures the amount of time the sales professional spends actively engaged in selling activities.
✓ Lead Response Time: Evaluates the speed at which the sales professional responds to incoming leads or inquiries.
✓ Sales Activity Ratio: Calculates the ratio of selling activities to non-selling activities.

These are just a few examples of KPIs that can be set for sales professionals. It's important to choose KPIs that align with the organization's goals and objectives, as well as the specific responsibilities and focus of the sales team. Additionally, KPIs should be SMART (Specific, Measurable, Achievable, Relevant, Time-bound) to ensure they are meaningful and actionable.

Monitoring Sales Metrics and Targets

By tracking key metrics and setting targets, sales managers can gain valuable insights into the effectiveness of their sales efforts, identify areas for improvement, and take proactive measures to achieve desired outcomes.

1. Selecting Relevant Sales Metrics:

- ✓ Identify the sales metrics that are most relevant to the organization's objectives and sales strategy.
- ✓ Consider metrics such as revenue, conversion rates, average deal size, sales cycle length, and customer acquisition cost.
- ✓ Ensure that the selected metrics provide a comprehensive view of the sales process and performance.

Example: To effectively monitor sales performance, it is essential to select relevant sales metrics that align with the organization's objectives and sales strategy. Key metrics may include revenue, conversion rates, average deal size, sales cycle length, and customer acquisition cost. These metrics provide insights into the effectiveness and efficiency of the sales process, allowing sales managers to assess performance accurately.

2. Setting Clear Targets:

- ✓ Establish specific and measurable targets for each sales metric.
- ✓ Ensure that targets are realistic, achievable, and aligned with the organization's overall goals.
- ✓ Consider historical performance, industry benchmarks, and market conditions when setting targets.

Example: Clear targets must be set for each sales metric to provide a benchmark for performance evaluation. These targets should be specific, measurable, and aligned with the organization's overall goals. Taking into account historical performance, industry benchmarks, and market conditions helps ensure that targets are realistic and achievable.

3. Implementing Tracking and Reporting Systems:
- ✓ Utilize technology and sales tools to track and collect data on sales metrics.
- ✓ Implement a centralized reporting system to monitor and analyze sales performance.
- ✓ Ensure that the tracking and reporting systems provide real-time data and are accessible to relevant stakeholders.

Example: Implementing robust tracking and reporting systems is crucial for effective sales performance management. Leveraging technology and sales tools, such as customer relationship management (CRM) software, allows for the collection and organization of sales data. A centralized reporting system provides real-time insights into sales metrics and performance, enabling sales managers to make informed decisions and take timely action.

4. Regular Performance Review and Analysis:
- ✓ Conduct regular reviews of sales performance against set targets.
- ✓ Analyze trends, patterns, and deviations from expected outcomes.
- ✓ Identify areas of improvement and develop action plans to address performance gaps.

Example: Regular performance reviews are vital to monitor sales performance and ensure alignment with targets. Analyzing trends, patterns, and deviations from expected outcomes provides insights into the effectiveness of sales strategies and tactics. Identifying areas of improvement and developing action plans allows sales managers to proactively address performance gaps and drive continuous improvement.

5. Providing Feedback and Coaching:
- ✓ Provide timely and constructive feedback to sales professionals based on performance metrics.
- ✓ Offer coaching and support to help sales professionals improve their performance.
- ✓ Use performance data to identify training and development needs and tailor coaching programs accordingly.

Example: Using performance metrics as a foundation, sales managers can provide timely and constructive feedback to sales professionals. By leveraging performance data, they can identify strengths, weaknesses, and areas for improvement. Offering personalized coaching and support helps sales professionals enhance their skills and achieve their targets.

By effectively monitoring sales metrics and targets, sales managers can gain insights into the performance of their sales team, identify areas for improvement, and take proactive measures to optimize sales performance and drive success.

Conducting Performance Reviews and Assessments

This part focuses on the crucial aspect of conducting performance reviews and assessments to effectively manage and evaluate sales performance. Regular performance reviews provide an opportunity to assess individual sales team members, provide feedback, and align performance with organizational goals. This chapter explores the steps involved in conducting performance reviews and offers examples to guide the process.

1. Establish Performance Review Criteria:

- ✓ Define Key Performance Indicators (KPIs): Determine the specific metrics and goals that are relevant to each sales role, such as revenue targets, conversion rates, or customer satisfaction.
- ✓ Align with Organizational Objectives: Ensure that the performance review criteria are aligned with the overall objectives of the sales team and the organization as a whole.
- ✓ Use Objective and Subjective Measures: Combine quantitative data with qualitative assessments to provide a comprehensive evaluation of sales performance.

Example: When conducting performance reviews, sales managers should establish clear criteria that align with the goals of the sales team. For example, if the organization aims to increase revenue by 20% in the next quarter, the performance review criteria may include individual revenue targets as a key measure of success.

2. Prepare for Performance Review Meetings:

- ✓ Gather Performance Data: Collect relevant performance data, such as sales figures, customer feedback, and any other metrics or indicators that are part of the performance review criteria.
- ✓ Review Individual Goals and Objectives: Assess each sales team member's individual goals and objectives to evaluate their progress and achievement.
- ✓ Solicit Feedback: Seek input from colleagues, clients, or other team members who have

worked closely with the sales professional being reviewed.

Example: Before conducting performance review meetings, sales managers should gather all the necessary performance data and review the individual goals and objectives set for each sales team member. Additionally, gathering feedback from colleagues and clients provides valuable insights into the sales professional's performance and contribution.

3. Conduct the Performance Review Meeting:

- ✓ Provide Clear Expectations: Clearly communicate the purpose and structure of the performance review meeting to the sales professional being reviewed.
- ✓ Discuss Performance Data: Present the performance data and metrics, highlighting both areas of strength and areas that need improvement.
- ✓ Offer Constructive Feedback: Provide specific examples and observations to support the feedback and identify areas where the sales professional can enhance their performance.
- ✓ Set Development Goals: Collaborate with the sales professional to set actionable and measurable goals for improvement and development.

Example: During the performance review meeting, sales managers should ensure that the purpose and structure of the meeting are clear. By discussing performance data and metrics, providing constructive feedback with specific examples, and collaboratively setting development goals, sales managers can facilitate a productive and meaningful conversation about performance.

4. Create an Action Plan:
- ✓ Develop Individual Development Plans: Work with the sales professional to create an action plan that outlines specific steps and strategies for improving performance.
- ✓ Provide Resources and Support: Identify resources, training programs, or coaching opportunities that can help the sales professional address their areas for improvement.
- ✓ Set Performance Review Timeline: Establish a timeline for future performance reviews and clarify the expectations for progress and follow-up.

Example: To support the growth and development of sales professionals, sales managers should collaborate with them to create individual development plans. This may include recommending relevant training programs or providing resources to enhance specific skills. Additionally, establishing a timeline for future performance reviews helps maintain accountability and provides a framework for tracking progress.

Conducting performance reviews and assessments allows sales managers to evaluate individual sales performance, provide feedback, and identify areas for improvement. By following a structured approach and providing actionable feedback, sales managers can help sales professionals reach their full potential and contribute to the overall success of the sales team and the organization.

Conducting Performance Reviews and Assessments for Sales

Performance reviews and assessments are essential tools for evaluating the performance of sales professionals and providing valuable feedback. This process allows sales managers to assess individual sales team members, identify areas of improvement, and align performance with organizational goals. In this chapter, we will explore the complete details of conducting performance reviews and assessments for sales, including the steps involved and examples to guide the process.

1. Establish Performance Review Criteria:

- ✓ Define Key Performance Indicators (KPIs): Determine the specific metrics and goals that are relevant to each sales role, such as revenue targets, conversion rates, or customer satisfaction.
- ✓ Align with Organizational Objectives: Ensure that the performance review criteria are aligned with the overall objectives of the sales team and the organization as a whole.
- ✓ Use Objective and Subjective Measures: Combine quantitative data with qualitative assessments to provide a comprehensive evaluation of sales performance.

Example: In a performance review, key performance indicators for a sales representative may include monthly sales targets, conversion rates, customer retention rates, and feedback from customers regarding their satisfaction with the sales process.

2. Prepare for Performance Review Meetings:

- ✓ Gather Performance Data: Collect relevant performance data, such as sales figures, customer feedback, and any other metrics or indicators that are part of the performance review criteria.

- ✓ Review Individual Goals and Objectives: Assess each sales team member's individual goals and objectives to evaluate their progress and achievement.
- ✓ Solicit Feedback: Seek input from colleagues, clients, or other team members who have worked closely with the sales professional being reviewed.

Example: Before the performance review meeting, the sales manager collects data on the sales representative's performance, including sales figures, client feedback, and progress towards individual goals. They may also request feedback from colleagues or clients who have interacted with the sales representative.

3. Conduct the Performance Review Meeting:

- ✓ Provide Clear Expectations: Clearly communicate the purpose and structure of the performance review meeting to the sales professional being reviewed.
- ✓ Discuss Performance Data: Present the performance data and metrics, highlighting both areas of strength and areas that need improvement.
- ✓ Offer Constructive Feedback: Provide specific examples and observations to support the feedback and identify areas where the sales professional can enhance their performance.
- ✓ Set Development Goals: Collaborate with the sales professional to set actionable and measurable goals for improvement and development.

Example: During the performance review meeting, the sales manager explains the purpose of the review and goes over the performance data, discussing both positive achievements and areas that need improvement. They provide constructive feedback, such as highlighting successful sales strategies used by the sales representative or suggesting areas where they can improve their closing techniques. Together, they set goals for the upcoming period, such as increasing monthly sales by a specific percentage or improving client relationship management skills.

4. Create an Action Plan:

- ✓ Develop Individual Development Plans: Work with the sales professional to create an action plan that outlines specific steps and strategies for improving performance.
- ✓ Provide Resources and Support: Identify resources, training programs, or coaching opportunities that can help the sales professional address their areas for improvement.
- ✓ Set Performance Review Timeline: Establish a timeline for future performance reviews and clarify the expectations for progress and follow-up.

Example: The sales manager collaborates with the sales professional to create an individual development plan that includes activities such as attending sales training workshops, shadowing successful sales team members, or participating in role-playing exercises. They provide resources and support by sharing relevant articles, recommending sales books, or offering coaching sessions. They also set a timeline for regular check-ins and performance reviews to monitor progress and provide ongoing support.

Conducting performance reviews and assessments enables sales managers to evaluate individual sales performance, provide feedback, and identify areas for improvement. By following a structured approach and providing actionable feedback, sales managers can help sales professionals reach their full potential and contribute to the overall success of the sales team and the organization.

Addressing Underperformance and Coaching Needs

In this section, we will explore the complete details of how to address underperformance and meet coaching needs effectively. We will discuss the steps involved in addressing underperformance, providing coaching, and offering support to help sales professionals improve their performance and achieve their full potential.

1. Identify Underperformance:
- ✓ Monitor Key Performance Indicators (KPIs): Regularly review sales metrics and targets to identify any significant gaps or areas of underperformance.
- ✓ Analyze Performance Data: Examine sales reports, conversion rates, revenue figures, and other relevant data to identify trends and patterns that indicate underperformance.
- ✓ Seek Feedback: Gather input from colleagues, clients, or other team members who have interacted with the sales professional to gain additional insights.

Example: Sales manager reviews sales reports and notices a consistent decline in monthly sales figures for a particular sales representative. The conversion rate has also decreased, and clients have provided feedback about a lack of follow-up and poor communication.

2. Assess the Root Causes of Underperformance:

✓ Conduct Performance Discussions: Schedule a meeting with the sales professional to discuss their performance and understand the factors contributing to underperformance.

✓ Identify Skill Gaps: Determine if underperformance is due to a lack of specific skills, knowledge, or experience.

✓ Consider External Factors: Assess if external factors, such as market changes or product-related challenges, are affecting the sales professional's performance.

Example: During a performance discussion, the sales manager learns that the underperforming sales representative lacks confidence in handling objections and struggles with closing deals. They also mention that recent changes in the market have made it more challenging to generate leads.

3. Provide Targeted Coaching and Support:

✓ Develop a Coaching Plan: Create a tailored coaching plan that focuses on addressing the identified skill gaps and challenges.

✓ Offer Training and Development Opportunities: Provide relevant training programs, workshops, or resources to enhance the sales professional's skills and knowledge.

✓ Schedule Regular Coaching Sessions: Set up regular coaching sessions to monitor progress, provide guidance, and offer ongoing support.

Example: The sales manager creates a coaching plan that includes targeted training sessions on objection handling techniques and effective closing strategies. They recommend a sales training workshop and provide online resources for further learning. They schedule weekly coaching sessions to review progress, offer feedback, and address any questions or concerns.

4. Set Performance Improvement Goals:

- ✓ Collaborate on Performance Goals: Work together with the sales professional to establish specific, measurable, attainable, relevant, and time-bound (SMART) goals for performance improvement.
- ✓ Break Down Goals into Actionable Steps: Help the sales professional identify actionable steps and milestones to achieve their performance improvement goals.
- ✓ Provide Regular Feedback: Offer ongoing feedback and guidance to keep the sales professional focused and motivated.

Example: The sales manager and sales representative collaborate to set SMART goals, such as increasing monthly sales by 20% within the next quarter. They break down the goal into actionable steps, such as improving objection handling techniques, implementing a consistent follow-up process, and enhancing product knowledge. The sales manager provides regular feedback on the sales representative's progress and offers suggestions for improvement.

5. Monitor and Evaluate Progress:

- ✓ Track Performance Metrics: Continuously monitor performance metrics to assess progress towards improvement goals.
- ✓ Conduct Check-In Meetings: Schedule regular check-in meetings to discuss progress,

address challenges, and make any necessary adjustments to the coaching plan.
- ✓ Celebrate Achievements: Recognize and celebrate milestones and achievements along the way to maintain motivation and engagement.

Example: The sales manager tracks the sales representative's performance metrics, such as monthly sales figures and conversion rates, to evaluate progress. They conduct bi-weekly check-in meetings to discuss challenges, provide guidance, and modify the coaching plan if needed. When the sales representative achieves a significant increase in monthly sales, the manager celebrates their success and acknowledges their efforts.

Addressing underperformance and coaching sales professionals are essential elements of managing and evaluating sales performance. By identifying underperformance, assessing root causes, providing targeted coaching and support, setting performance improvement goals, and monitoring progress, sales managers can effectively address underperformance and help sales professionals reach their full potential.

Continuously Improving Sales Processes and Strategies

We will now discuss how to evaluate and analyze sales processes, identify areas for improvement, implement changes, and measure the impact of those changes. By continuously refining sales processes and strategies, organizations can optimize sales performance, increase efficiency, and drive revenue growth.

1. Evaluate Current Sales Processes:

- ✓ Review the Sales Funnel: Assess each stage of the sales funnel, from lead generation to deal closure, to identify any bottlenecks or inefficiencies.
- ✓ Analyze Sales Data: Analyze sales metrics, conversion rates, and win/loss ratios to gain insights into the effectiveness of the current sales processes.
- ✓ Seek Feedback: Gather feedback from sales representatives, customers, and other stakeholders to understand their experiences and perspectives on the sales processes.

Example: A company reviews its sales funnel and identifies that a significant number of leads are dropping off at the qualification stage. The conversion rate from qualified leads to closed deals is lower than expected.

2. Identify Areas for Improvement:

- ✓ Identify Process Gaps: Identify specific areas within the sales processes that need improvement, such as lead qualification, sales messaging, or objection handling.
- ✓ Benchmark Best Practices: Research industry best practices and compare them to the current sales processes to identify gaps and opportunities for improvement.
- ✓ Consider Technology Solutions: Evaluate the use of sales tools, CRM systems, or automation software that can streamline and optimize the sales processes.

Example: After evaluating the sales processes, the company realizes that there is a lack of standardized qualification criteria for leads. Sales representatives have varying approaches to lead qualification, leading to inconsistencies in the quality of leads passed to the next stage.

3. Implement Changes and Strategies:

- ✓ Develop an Improvement Plan: Create a detailed plan outlining the specific changes and strategies to be implemented to address the identified areas for improvement.
- ✓ Communicate and Train: Communicate the changes to the sales team and provide necessary training and resources to ensure their understanding and adoption of the new processes.
- ✓ Test and Refine: Pilot the changes in a controlled environment and gather feedback from the sales team. Refine the processes based on feedback and iterate as necessary.

Example: The company develops a plan to standardize lead qualification criteria and create a clear process for qualifying leads. They communicate the changes to the sales team through a series of training sessions and provide them with guidelines and tools for effective lead qualification. The changes are piloted with a small group of sales representatives, and their feedback is collected to refine the new processes.

4. Measure and Monitor Performance:

- ✓ Define Key Performance Indicators (KPIs): Establish KPIs that align with the improved sales processes and strategies, such as conversion rates, average deal size, or sales cycle length.
- ✓ Implement Tracking and Reporting Systems: Utilize CRM systems or sales analytics tools to track and report on the identified KPIs.

✓ Regularly Review and Analyze Data: Review the performance data regularly to evaluate the impact of the changes and identify any further areas for improvement.

Example: The company sets KPIs related to lead conversion rates, average deal size, and sales cycle length. They implement a CRM system that allows them to track and analyze the performance data. They review the data on a monthly basis and observe an improvement in lead conversion rates and a reduction in the sales cycle length, indicating the positive impact of the implemented changes.

5. Foster a Culture of Continuous Improvement:

✓ Encourage Feedback: Create a culture where sales representatives are encouraged to provide feedback and suggestions for further process improvements.

✓ Promote Collaboration: Foster collaboration between sales representatives, managers, and other departments to share best practices and innovative ideas.

✓ Regularly Evaluate and Adjust: Continuously evaluate the effectiveness of the sales processes and strategies and make adjustments based on market dynamics and changing business needs.

Example: The company establishes a feedback mechanism where sales representatives can share their ideas for process improvement. They conduct regular team meetings to discuss challenges and success stories, promoting collaboration and knowledge sharing. They also conduct periodic reviews of the sales processes to ensure they remain aligned with the evolving market conditions.

Continuous improvement of sales processes and strategies is vital for achieving and sustaining sales success. By evaluating current sales processes, identifying areas for improvement, implementing changes, measuring performance, and fostering a culture of continuous improvement, organizations can enhance sales performance, increase efficiency, and drive revenue growth. This iterative approach ensures that the sales team remains adaptable, responsive to market dynamics, and consistently delivers exceptional results.

Chapter 11
Future Trends and Conclusion

Future Trends and Conclusion

The Continuous Evolution of Sales Hiring

In this final chapter, we will reflect on the key insights gained throughout the book and explore the future trends and advancements in the field of sales hiring. We will emphasize the importance of adapting to changing market dynamics, embracing technology, and continuously evolving recruitment strategies to stay ahead in the competitive landscape.

Recap of Key Learnings:

- ✓ Emphasize the importance of hiring top-performing sales professionals and the impact they have on business success.
- ✓ Understand the sales hiring process, including assessing the current sales team, defining job requirements, sourcing candidates, and conducting effective interviews.
- ✓ Create compelling job descriptions that attract the right candidates and align with the organization's sales objectives.
- ✓ Implement a structured interview process to assess candidates' skills, competencies, motivation, and fit with the organization.
- ✓ Make informed decisions about compensation packages, offers, and negotiation strategies.
- ✓ Develop an effective on-boarding and training process to set new hires up for success.
- ✓ Implement strategies for retaining top sales talent, such as creating a positive sales culture, offering career development opportunities, and providing performance feedback and recognition.

- ✓ Continuously monitor and evaluate sales performance through key performance indicators, metrics, and performance reviews.
- ✓ Constantly strive for improvement by identifying and addressing areas of underperformance, refining sales processes, and embracing new technologies.

Future Trends in Sales Hiring:

- ✓ Use of Artificial Intelligence (AI) and Predictive Analytics: AI can streamline candidate screening, improve the selection process, and predict sales success based on data analysis.
- ✓ Virtual and Remote Hiring: Remote work and virtual interviews have become more prevalent, allowing organizations to access a broader talent pool and enhance flexibility in the hiring process.
- ✓ Focus on Diversity and Inclusion: Organizations are placing increased emphasis on diversifying their sales teams to bring in different perspectives and enhance customer engagement.
- ✓ Skills-based Assessments: Assessments focused on specific sales skills and competencies are gaining popularity to ensure candidates possess the necessary capabilities for success in the role.
- ✓ Continuous Learning and Development: Sales professionals are expected to embrace lifelong learning, and organizations are investing in continuous training and development programs to keep their teams up to date with industry trends and customer needs.

- ✓ Employer Branding and Candidate Experience: Companies are paying more attention to their employer brand and ensuring a positive candidate experience throughout the hiring process to attract and retain top sales talent.

Example: A sales organization embraces AI technology to automate the initial screening process. The AI system analyzes candidate resumes, assesses their qualifications and experience, and provides a shortlist of top candidates based on predetermined criteria. This saves time and allows recruiters to focus on evaluating candidates who are the best fit for the role.

The world of sales hiring is continuously evolving, driven by changing market dynamics, advancements in technology, and shifting candidate expectations. By staying abreast of industry trends, embracing new recruitment strategies, and adapting to the ever-changing landscape, organizations can attract, hire, and retain top sales talent. The continuous evolution of sales hiring is not only essential for business success but also an opportunity to stay ahead of the competition and drive sustainable growth. By leveraging the knowledge gained from this book and embracing future trends, organizations can build high-performing sales teams that propel them towards long-term success.

Embracing Technology and Artificial Intelligence

We will explore how AI can revolutionize candidate sourcing, screening, assessment, and decision-making, leading to more efficient and effective hiring outcomes. We will also discuss the potential benefits and challenges associated with integrating AI into sales hiring practices.

The Role of Technology in Sales Hiring:

- ✓ AI-powered Sourcing: AI tools can analyze vast amounts of data from various sources, such as online platforms and social media, to identify and attract potential sales candidates who match the desired criteria.
- ✓ Automated Screening: AI algorithms can quickly analyze resumes, applications, and online profiles to screen candidates based on predefined qualifications, saving time and effort in the initial screening process.
- ✓ Predictive Analytics: AI can analyze historical data on successful sales hires and identify patterns and characteristics associated with high performance. This data-driven approach helps predict a candidate's potential success in the sales role.
- ✓ Virtual Interviews: Technology enables virtual interviews, eliminating geographical limitations and allowing organizations to reach a wider pool of candidates. Video conferencing tools facilitate face-to-face interviews, fostering better candidate engagement and assessment.
- ✓ AI-based Assessments: AI-powered assessments can evaluate sales skills, cognitive abilities, and personality traits. These assessments provide valuable insights into a candidate's suitability for the sales role.
- ✓ Decision Support Systems: AI can provide data-driven insights and recommendations to aid in the final hiring decision-making process. These systems consider various factors, such

as candidate performance in assessments, interview evaluations, and comparative analysis with existing top performers.

Example: An organization adopts an AI-powered candidate sourcing platform that scans various online job boards, professional networks, and social media platforms to identify potential sales candidates. The platform uses machine learning algorithms to analyze candidate profiles and match them with the organization's specific requirements. This significantly reduces the time and effort involved in manual candidate sourcing and expands the talent pool.

Benefits and Challenges of AI in Sales Hiring:

Benefits:

- Increased Efficiency: AI automates time-consuming tasks, allowing recruiters to focus on higher-value activities.
- Enhanced Candidate Experience: AI-powered tools streamline the hiring process, providing faster responses and personalized interactions, which improves the candidate experience.
- Improved Decision-making: AI algorithms analyze data objectively and provide insights that support more informed hiring decisions.
- Scalability: AI technology can handle large volumes of data, enabling organizations to manage a high volume of candidates efficiently.

Challenges:

- Bias in Algorithms: AI systems may inadvertently perpetuate biases if not carefully designed and monitored. Organizations need to ensure fairness and avoid discriminatory practices.

- Data Privacy and Security: With the increased use of technology and data, it is crucial to address concerns related to data privacy and security to protect sensitive candidate information.
- Human Touch: While AI can enhance the hiring process, it is essential to maintain human interaction and judgment in assessing soft skills and cultural fit.

Example: An organization adopts an AI-powered assessment tool that analyzes candidates' responses to situational and behavioral questions. While the tool provides objective insights into a candidate's skills and competencies, the organization ensures that the final hiring decision involves human evaluation to consider intangible factors such as cultural fit and emotional intelligence.

Embracing technology, particularly AI, in the sales hiring process offers significant advantages, including increased efficiency, improved decision-making, and enhanced candidate experiences. However, organizations must carefully navigate the challenges associated with AI, such as bias and data privacy, to ensure fair and ethical hiring practices. By embracing technology and leveraging AI's capabilities, organizations can stay ahead of the curve, attract top sales talent, and make data-driven decisions that drive business success. The future of sales hiring lies in the effective integration of technology, enabling organizations to optimize their hiring outcomes and adapt to the evolving landscape of talent acquisition.

Predictive Analytics and Sales Talent Acquisition

We will now explore the role of predictive analytics in sales talent acquisition and discuss how it can revolutionize the way organizations identify, attract, and hire top sales professionals. We will delve into the benefits of using predictive analytics in the hiring process and discuss its potential applications in assessing candidate fit, improving retention, and driving overall sales performance. Additionally, we will examine the challenges and considerations associated with implementing predictive analytics in sales talent acquisition.

The Power of Predictive Analytics in Sales Hiring:

- Talent Identification: Predictive analytics leverages historical data, performance metrics, and behavioral patterns to identify the key characteristics and traits of successful sales professionals. By analyzing this data, organizations can identify and target candidates who exhibit similar attributes, increasing the likelihood of hiring top performers.
- Candidate Assessment: Predictive analytics enables organizations to assess candidate fit by analyzing various data points such as resumes, assessments, social media profiles, and interview feedback. This data-driven approach provides insights into a candidate's potential for success in the sales role and helps make informed hiring decisions.
- Retention and Performance Improvement: Predictive analytics can identify factors that contribute to employee turnover and low sales performance. By analyzing data on tenure,

sales results, and other relevant metrics, organizations can proactively address retention challenges and design strategies to enhance sales performance.

- Personalized Development: Predictive analytics can identify skill gaps and development needs of sales professionals. By leveraging this data, organizations can provide targeted training and development opportunities that align with individual strengths and weaknesses, maximizing employee potential and driving continuous improvement.

Example: A sales organization implements a predictive analytics tool that analyzes various data sources, including historical sales data, candidate profiles, and assessments. By identifying patterns and characteristics associated with top performers, the tool helps recruiters identify candidates who are likely to succeed in the sales role. This data-driven approach improves the accuracy of candidate assessment and selection.

Benefits and Challenges of Predictive Analytics in Sales Talent Acquisition:

Benefits:

- ✓ Enhanced Hiring Accuracy: Predictive analytics enables organizations to make more accurate predictions about candidate performance and fit, leading to better hiring decisions and increased success rates.
- ✓ Efficient Resource Allocation: By leveraging data and analytics, organizations can optimize their recruitment efforts, focusing on candidates with the highest potential for success, thus saving time and resources.

- ✓ Improved Retention: Predictive analytics can identify factors that contribute to turnover and help organizations develop targeted retention strategies, resulting in higher employee satisfaction and longer tenures.
- ✓ Data-Driven Decision Making: Predictive analytics provides objective insights that support decision-making throughout the hiring process, reducing biases and improving overall hiring outcomes.

Challenges:

- ✓ Data Quality and Availability: Implementing predictive analytics relies on access to high-quality and relevant data. Organizations must ensure data integrity, accuracy, and compliance with privacy regulations.
- ✓ Algorithm Bias: There is a risk of algorithmic biases when developing predictive models. Organizations must carefully design and monitor the models to avoid perpetuating bias in the hiring process.
- ✓ Change Management: Implementing predictive analytics requires a cultural shift and change management strategies to ensure adoption and acceptance among stakeholders.
- ✓ Ethical Considerations: The use of predictive analytics raises ethical concerns, such as the appropriate use of candidate data and maintaining transparency in the decision-making process.

Example: A technology company incorporates predictive analytics into its sales talent acquisition process. By analyzing historical data, performance metrics, and candidate profiles, the organization identifies patterns and characteristics associated with successful sales professionals. The insights gained from predictive analytics help recruiters make data-driven decisions and select candidates with a higher likelihood of driving sales success.

Predictive analytics offers immense potential in revolutionizing the sales talent acquisition process. By harnessing the power of data and analytics, organizations can make more informed decisions, increase hiring accuracy, improve retention rates, and drive overall sales performance. However, it is crucial for organizations to address challenges related to data quality, algorithm bias, change management, and ethics to ensure the ethical and effective implementation of predictive analytics in sales talent acquisition.

As the landscape of sales evolves, embracing predictive analytics in talent acquisition will become increasingly crucial for organizations to stay competitive and secure top sales talent. By leveraging the insights provided by predictive analytics, organizations can gain a strategic advantage in identifying, attracting, and retaining the best sales professionals in an ever-evolving marketplace.

Adapting to Changing Market Dynamics

In this final part, we will explore the importance of adapting to changing market dynamics in sales talent acquisition. We will discuss the impact of market trends on the hiring process and how organizations can stay ahead by embracing emerging practices and technologies. Additionally, we will examine the key considerations and strategies for effectively adapting to changing market dynamics in sales talent acquisition.

1. Understanding Changing Market Dynamics:

- ✓ Evolving Customer Needs: Market dynamics are constantly shaped by changing customer preferences and needs. Organizations must understand these shifts to align their sales talent acquisition strategies with the evolving demands of the market.
- ✓ Technological Advancements: The rise of technology has transformed the sales landscape, with tools like artificial intelligence, automation, and data analytics becoming integral to sales processes. Organizations need to embrace these technologies and adapt their talent acquisition strategies to attract candidates with the required digital skills and competencies.
- ✓ Globalization and Market Expansion: Globalization has expanded the reach of sales organizations, requiring them to hire sales professionals with cross-cultural understanding and the ability to navigate diverse markets. Organizations must adapt their talent acquisition strategies to attract candidates with global experience and a multicultural mindset.

Example: A software company operating in the tech industry recognizes the growing demand for cloud-based solutions. To adapt to this market trend, the organization adjusts its talent acquisition strategy to prioritize candidates with experience in cloud technologies and a deep understanding of the specific needs and challenges of cloud-based sales. This proactive approach helps the company attract top sales professionals who can effectively address the evolving market demands.

2. Embracing Emerging Practices and Technologies:

- ✓ Agile Talent Acquisition: Organizations need to adopt agile practices in talent acquisition, such as continuous candidate sourcing, streamlined interview processes, and rapid decision-making. This agility allows organizations to adapt quickly to market changes and secure top sales talent before their competitors.
- ✓ Digital Recruitment Platforms: Utilizing digital recruitment platforms, such as online job boards, social media, and professional networks, enables organizations to reach a broader pool of candidates and engage with them effectively. These platforms provide opportunities for targeted candidate sourcing and efficient communication throughout the hiring process.
- ✓ Virtual Hiring and On-boarding: With the increasing acceptance of remote work, organizations should leverage virtual hiring and on-boarding practices. Conducting video interviews, virtual assessments, and remote on-boarding programs allow organizations to tap into talent from anywhere, overcoming geographical limitations.

Example: A retail organization shifts its talent acquisition strategy to focus more on online channels and digital recruitment platforms. They leverage social media platforms and online job boards to promote their sales roles and engage with a broader range of candidates. Additionally, the organization implements virtual hiring practices, conducting video interviews and virtual assessments to streamline the hiring process and attract candidates from different locations.

Adapting to changing market dynamics is crucial for organizations to remain competitive in sales talent acquisition. By understanding market trends, embracing emerging practices and technologies, and proactively adjusting their talent acquisition strategies, organizations can attract top sales professionals who possess the skills, competencies, and adaptability needed to thrive in a rapidly evolving sales landscape. Continuous monitoring of market dynamics and proactive adjustments to talent acquisition strategies will position organizations for long-term success in acquiring and retaining top sales talent.

The Future of Hiring Top Performing Sales Talent

Finally, we will look at the future of hiring top performing sales talent. We will delve into emerging trends, technologies, and strategies that will shape the way organizations attract, assess, and retain sales professionals. Understanding these future trends will help organizations stay ahead of the curve and secure the best sales talent in a competitive marketplace.

Remote and Flexible Work: The future of work is increasingly becoming remote and flexible. Organizations need to adapt their talent acquisition strategies to attract sales professionals who thrive in remote environments and are comfortable with flexible work arrangements. Remote work opens up opportunities to tap into a global talent pool and provides flexibility to sales professionals, resulting in increased job satisfaction and productivity.

Example: A technology company embraces remote work and offers flexible work arrangements to its sales team. They leverage virtual collaboration tools, remote sales enablement programs, and virtual team-building activities to ensure seamless communication and collaboration. This approach enables the organization to attract top sales talent from around the world and retain high-performing professionals seeking flexibility in their work.

Data-Driven Decision Making: The future of hiring top sales talent lies in data-driven decision making. Organizations will increasingly leverage data analytics, artificial intelligence, and machine learning to identify patterns, predict success factors, and make informed hiring decisions. Data-driven insights will help organizations identify the most effective sourcing channels, assess candidate fit, and design personalized on-boarding and development programs.

Example: A pharmaceutical company implements a data-driven approach to hiring top performing sales talent. They analyze historical sales data, customer feedback, and market trends to identify the key attributes and skills that contribute to sales success. By integrating this data into their candidate assessment process, they can identify candidates who align with these success factors and have a higher probability of achieving sales targets.

Employer Branding and Employee Value Proposition: In the future, employer branding will play a crucial role in attracting top sales talent. Organizations need to differentiate themselves as desirable employers by showcasing their unique culture, values, career growth opportunities, and employee benefits. Building a strong employer brand and an attractive employee value proposition will attract top performers who align with the organization's values and vision.

Example: A retail organization invests in employer branding initiatives to position itself as an employer of choice for sales professionals. They highlight their employee development programs, recognition initiatives, and work-life balance policies through social media campaigns, employer review platforms, and industry events. As a result, they attract high-caliber sales candidates who are motivated by the organization's strong employee value proposition.

The future of hiring top performing sales talent is evolving rapidly. Embracing remote work, leveraging data-driven decision making, and investing in employer branding will be essential for organizations to attract and retain the best sales professionals. By staying ahead of emerging trends and adapting their talent acquisition strategies accordingly, organizations can gain a competitive edge in securing top performing sales talent, driving sales growth, and achieving long-term success in the dynamic sales landscape.

Conclusion

Congratulations! You have reached the end of **'Hiring Sales Winners:** *The Ultimate Guide to Hiring Top Performing Sales Talent!'* We hope that this comprehensive guide has equipped you with the knowledge, strategies, and practical tools to revolutionize your sales hiring process and build a team of exceptional sales professionals.

Throughout this book, we have explored every aspect of hiring top performing sales talent, from understanding the importance of hiring sales professionals to assessing your current team, defining your hiring strategy, creating effective job descriptions, sourcing candidates, conducting interviews, making compelling offers, on-boarding and training new hires, retaining top talent, managing and evaluating performance, and adapting to future trends.

By implementing the strategies and best practices outlined in this guide, you are well-positioned to attract, assess, and hire sales professionals who will not only meet but exceed your organization's sales targets and drive sustainable growth. You have learned how to craft compelling job descriptions that accurately outline the role, responsibilities, and desired skills. You have discovered various sourcing methods, from traditional channels to leveraging online platforms and social media. You have honed your interview skills, effectively assessing candidates' motivation, drive, experience, and skills through behavioral and situational interviews. You have mastered the art of making compelling job offers, negotiating salaries and commission structures, and handling counteroffers and conflicts. You have also gained insights into the critical importance of on-boarding, training, mentorship, and coaching to ensure the success of new hires. Moreover, this guide has highlighted the significance of creating a positive sales culture, offering career development opportunities, providing performance feedback and recognition, implementing incentives and rewards programs, and continuously improving sales processes and strategies to retain top sales talent and maximize their potential.

As we conclude, it is important to remember that the world of sales and recruitment is ever-evolving. The landscape is shaped by advancements in technology, the rise of artificial intelligence, the emergence of predictive analytics, and the need to adapt to changing market dynamics. It is crucial to embrace these changes, stay updated with the latest trends, and continuously evolve your hiring strategies to remain competitive and attract the best talent. We hope that this guide has not only provided you with actionable insights but has also ignited your passion for hiring sales winners. With dedication, perseverance, and the knowledge gained from this book, you are well-equipped to build a sales team that will drive your organization's success and propel it into the future.

Remember, hiring top performing sales talent is a continuous journey. Keep refining your processes, stay open to learning, and be proactive in your approach. The world of sales awaits, and with the right team by your side, there are no limits to what you can achieve.

Best of luck in your quest to hire sales winners and create a sales powerhouse!

About the Author
'GERARD ASSEY'

Gerard Assey is a Graduate in Economics, a PGD in Management (HRD) and holds a Doctorate in Leadership. Gerard holds several International Qualifications in Sales, Debt Collection, Training & Teaching, and is a 'Fellow' of the prestigious 'Institute of Sales & Marketing Management'-UK, a Certified NLP Practitioner, a 'Certified Trainer', an 'Accredited Management Teacher-Behavioral Sciences', a 'Certified Competency Facilitator', a 'Certified Management Consultant'- (the International credentials of a professional management consultant, awarded in accordance with global standards of the ICMCI); and a Certification from the University of Michigan in 'Successful Negotiation: Essential Strategies and Skills'

He is also a Member of the 'National Association of Sales Professionals' backed with several years experience in varied industries, both in India and Overseas. He also holds an 'Etiquette Consultant' Certification from the USA (by Sue Fox, Author of Best Seller: 'Business Etiquette for Dummies'. She has trained some of the top celebrities' world over). He was also a recipient of a scholarship for extensive training in Japan on 'Corporate Management for India'.

Gerard Assey is 'Founder & Chief Corporate Trainer' of the Group: **Citius, Altius, Fortius Unlimited**'- an organization that **celebrated 20 years of Glorious Service** in 2021, focusing on 3 Core Competencies:

People. Performance. Profit; in functional areas of Sales & Marketing, HR & Organizational Development, covering Recruitment, Training & Consultancy!

Having managed organizations with large Sales Forces in India & Overseas, his specialization cover extensive areas of Sales Training (All levels - Presentation, Negotiation, Key/ Strategic Accounts Management & Managerial Skills for all sectors), Bid Proposal/ Capture Planning/ Management Trainings, Retail Sales, Customer Service & Customer Retention Programs, Training for Prevention & Collection of Debt, Self & Personal Development Programs (Time Management, Teamwork & Team Building, Business Etiquette & Personal Grooming, Leadership & Managerial Skills, People Management Skills, Train-the-Trainer etc), including preparation of Custom-designed Business Manuals for Internal (HR, Induction, and Sales etc) & External use (Instruction, User Manuals).

Gerard has successfully conducted over 6000 Trainings & Workshops (as of Oct '23) all across India, Middle East, Africa, Europe & S.E. Asia. Besides public programs conducted regularly, both in India & Overseas, he has some of the top names as clients whom he services from Single Owners to large Public & Government undertakings, covering all sectors, for their in-house needs.

His website: www.CollectionSkills.com is the only one in this part of the world to be featured in the 'Collections & Credit Risk Magazine-USA' under 'Who's Who in Training' and ranks TOP, along with other websites listed below on most search engines.

Gerard is author of 81 books already (Oct 2023),

A few of the business related books being:

1. Bite-sized Bits on Commonsense Management
2. Heart to Heart on Life's Principles'
3. How to become a Successful Manager
4. The Sales Professionals' Master Workbook of S.Y.S.T.E.M.S
5. The Professional Business Email Etiquette Handbook & Guide
6. The Professional Business Video-Conferencing Etiquette Handbook & Guide
7. Professional Presentation Skills
8. Exceptional Customer Service
9. Professional Tele-Marketing Skills
10. Professional Debt Collection Skills
11. The G.R.E.A.T. Sales & Service Workbook
12. Sales Training Advantage for Results (*The Ultimate Sales Training Manual to enable you stand out as a S.T.A.R.*)
13. CEO Daily Planner & Organizer
14. The Sales Professionals' Master Daily Planner
15. The Professional Debt Collector's Master Daily Planner
16. My Daily Planner & Organizer
17. MY EMERGENCY INFORMATION RECORD (Family Emergency & Peace of Mind Planner)
18. The Ultimate Therapist & Counselors Planner and Organizer
19. Building an Ethical Workplace
20. Managing Relationships at Work
21. Managing Business Meetings Effectively
22. Effective Delegation Skills
23. Goal Setting for Success
24. B2B Selling by Email
25. Professional Business Etiquette & Grooming
26. Dining Etiquette & Table Manners
27. Effective Networking Skills
28. Grooming, Etiquette & Manners for Teens, Young Adults & Future Leaders
29. Inter-Personal Skills

Besides regularly contributing to business & trade journals, including international ones such as the 'Creative Training Techniques' and the 'Sales News' of the U.S.A, He is also a member of several prestigious bodies & trade associations, having participated in many Conferences & Workshops in India & Overseas.

Prior to his last assignment of leading & managing a large MNC as head, Gerard had a 3-year stint in the Middle East as a Consultant with a leading British Consultancy Firm.

As the past 'Official Country Representative' for the International Business Award- 'THE STEVIES'-(the business world's own Oscar) for about 4 years- he ensured a few Indian companies that qualify for the same every year!

Gerard can be contacted at:

Email: training@Sales-Training.in, training@CollectionSkills.com

Websites:

www.Sales-Training.in
www.EtiquetteWorks.in
www.CollectionSkills.com
www.RetailSalesTraining.in
www.SalesTrainingIndia.com
www.ManualPreparation.com
www.TrainingWithPuppets.com
www.FirstContactAcademy.com
www.SalesAndMarketingRecruiter.com

Our TRAININGS & BOOKS that can help your team

- ✓ **Sales Effectiveness**: Selling Skills for any Sector: Service/ Logistics/ FMCG Realty/ Insurance & Finance/ Media/ SPA's, Health Clubs & Salons/ Key Account Management, Effective Negotiation Skills/ Bid & Proposal Management Skills/ Retail Sales Training: Any Sector (Auto, Jewelry, Clothing, Luxury etc)
- ✓ **Customer Service Skills**-Complaints Handling & Customer Retention
- ✓ **Debt Prevention & Collection Skills**
- ✓ **Etiquette & Grooming**
- ✓ **Leadership & Managerial Skills**
- ✓ **Self & Personal Development Skills**: Presentation Skills/ Effective Communication Skills/Business Proposal Writing Skills/ Problem Solving & Decision Making Skills/ Empowering Secretaries-The perfect PA! (For Secretaries & PA's)/ Effective Time Management/ Teamwork & Teambuilding/ P.R.I.D.E- **P**ersonal **R**esponsibility **I**n **D**elivering **E**xcellence

A Few of Our Business Books
By the Top Corporate Trainer & Author of 81 Books! (Oct '23)
And...DAILY PLANNERS for Every Corporate Need!
All Books available Online on all leading Stores in E-book & Paperback Formats
Experts in Training for over 22 years:
Sales, Debt Prevention & Collection, Etiquette & Grooming ,
Leadership & Managerial Skills, Self & Personal Development Programs
By the Top Corporate Trainer (Over 6000 workshops)
& Author of 81 Published Books (Oct'23)

9 789393 924902